It Is What It Is
Further Adventures of a Western Mystic

By Peter Mt. Shasta

Published by Church of the Seven Rays
PO Box 711, Mount Shasta, CA 96067
www.I-AM-Teachings.com

ISBN: 9781078474207

Copyright 2019, by Peter Mt. Shasta

No part of this book may be reproduced, stored in a retrieval system, or be transmitted by any means without the written permission of the author.

Other books by Peter Mt. Shasta:

"I AM" the Open Door

"I AM" Affirmations and the Secret of their Effective Use

"I AM" The Living Christ

"I AM" the Violet Tara

Search for the Guru:
Adventures of a Western Mystic, Book I

Apprentice to the Masters:
Adventures of a Western Mystic: Book II

My Search in Tibet for the Secret Wish-Fulfilling Jewel

Lady Master Pearl, My Teacher

Step By Step, Ascended Master Discourses

Let come what comes…let go what goes…
See what remains.

-Ramana Maharshi

Table of Contents

NOTE 9
FIRST EXPERIENCE OF SAMADHI 11
REALIZATION AT KNIFE POINT 13
BARNYARD SATCHITANANDA 17
DISAGREEMENT WITH SAINT GERMAIN 21
HOLDING THE FIELD 23
TAKING ON KARMA 31
FLYING 35
LOST OVER THE MOUNTAINS 39
FLYING BY INTUITION 41
PROTECTED BY SAINT GERMAIN 43
OVERCOMING SHYNESS 45
SKYDIVING 47
THE FLYING IMMORTALS 55
IDENTIFIED FLYING OBJECT 57
THE POWER OF PURITY 59
BABA VISITS IN A BMW 61
THE MASTERS SAVE ME AGAIN 65
ASCENSION OF MASTER HUILING 71
ADVENTURES OF MASTER YU 73

LEAVING MOUNT SHASTA	81
INVITATION FROM A DAKINI	85
COME ALONG	93
THE HOUR OF THE SPIDER	97
ECKHART TOLLE AT WALMART	103
A VISIT FROM TWO MASTERS	107
ZEN MECHANIC	111
MY SPACECRAFT	115
LOVE OPENS THE DOOR	117
THE MAN IN THE HOODIE	121
INTERNATIONAL VISITORS	125
MAHARAJJI APPEARS	127
THE PLACE OF GREAT AWAKENING	131
A CAT RETURNS A FAVOR	137
MY RESERVED SPACE	139
EMBRACING LIFE AS THE PATH	141
MY MOTHER RETURNS	149
SAINT GERMAIN SENDS A HELPER	153
LATTE ART	155
I AM GOD	157
THE CRYING BOWL	161
A TREE BEING	163

DOG WISDOM 165
DISAPPEARING WASPS 167
THE BOOK TITLE 169
WHOSE GAME IS IT? 171

Note

The experiences in this book are not all in chronological order as I did not want to burden the reader with long explanations. Hopefully, it is not the sequence that is important, but the essence.

Most names of people I mention have been changed to protect their privacy.

I would like to thank Juno Dawson for her generous and insightful help editing this edition.

First Experience of Samadhi[1]

During the yoga posture of *savasana*…I was catapulted out of my body into cosmic consciousness. Lying on my back in surrender, I lost awareness of self and merged with waves of light undulating through eternity. How long I was gone is a mystery. I only knew that to attain this transcendence of self would be my goal.

-Peter Mt. Shasta,
adapted from his autobiographical,
Search for the Guru: Adventures of a Western Mystic, Book I

---

[1] *Samadhi* (Sanskrit): Blissful merging of individual consciousness with absolute consciousness.

Realization at Knife Point

Three men held me at knife point near Tompkins Square on New York City's Lower East Side. After they emptied my wallet, I was enraged. *They have no right to do that…I will get a gun and make sure that never happens again!* I saw myself as another Charles Bronson in the film *Death Wish,* where a man becomes a vigilante after the murder of his wife.

I went back to my apartment and, desperate for guidance, read in the *I Ching,*

He who takes up the sword will die by the sword.

I realized I needed to deal with this consciously rather than react with violence. I had grown up in the affluent suburbs and never had to deal with violence outside of touch-football games during recess. Now, it was in my face.

I had begun taking yoga classes with Swami Satchitananda and studying Indian philosophy and thought, *perhaps if I generate enough light I will be protected.* I had read *Autobiography of a Yogi,* the classic book of Eastern spirituality where Yogananda tells of incidents where the light worked such miracles. That aspiration would soon be tested, for on my way home a few weeks later, I was again held up at knife point.

Entering the slum where I lived on Avenue B, a man who had been sitting on the garbage can beside the door followed me inside. He walked up the stairs behind me to my 5th floor flat and as I fiddled with the door key, he pulled out a knife. He was joined by another man who descended the stairs and also pulled out a knife. Pushed against the wall, I felt the point of a knife prick my abdomen through my shirt, while another one pushed against my right cheek.

"Open the door!" the one of them shouted.

I did as he ordered, and they followed me into my tiny flat.

"Sit down!" one ordered, holding his knife against my throat, while the other one looked around the room until his eyes settled on the stereo. As he began loading it into a bag, I remembered what I had read by Yogananda that desires and attachments are the cause of suffering. I had decided to get rid of some possessions. Had that been a premonition?

I was amazed at how surrendered I was to losing the stereo; I was more hurt at the uncaring way I was being "ripped off." I felt a part of me being taken without my consent. As I gazed at the floor, feeling the rise and fall of my chest, I thought, *God is in their hearts as well as mine; so, God, come into action here!*

The fear evaporated and I said, "This is not a good way to live! I don't like the way you are treating me. I try to help others. Why didn't you just ask me for what you need?"

"What?" the one packing up my stereo said in disbelief.

"Isn't there something else I can do that will be of more help to you? You are probably going to sell the stereo to buy drugs, and you will only get a fraction of what it's worth. Then, tomorrow you will need more money. Isn't there something else you need?"

The young man standing beside me lowered the knife, pulled up a chair and sat down next to me, while the other sat on the edge of my bed. Now I could see that they were just kids.

"Well, there is something I need," the one sitting on the bed said, "but I doubt you'd do it."

"What is it?"

"I need an operation and don't know anyone over 21 to sign me into the hospital."

"What about your parents?" I asked.

"My dad kicked me out and I been watchin' out for myself since I was 14. Now, I need this operation. The government will pay, but I need an adult to sign the admission form—someone to take responsibility for me."

"I'll take responsibility for you," I said.

"Man, you would do that for me?"

"Sure, just tell me where to meet you," I said.

I gave him a piece of paper and a pen and as he began to scrawl the address of the hospital, I suddenly felt him as a fellow human being—his basic goodness.

Barnyard Satchitananda

One spring, Peter Default invited me to visit him and his wife Ruth, at their farm in Hillsdale, New York for the weekend.[2] I had been cooped up in my tiny flat in New York City all winter and looked forward to sun and fresh air.

Friday night we sat around the dinner table in front of a roaring fire and as we sipped the tea Ruth made from her garden herbs, we chatted about poetry and politics. The tea was full of the spirit of the earth, and that night I slept in the embrace of Mother Earth.

I woke early, full of energy and eager for something to do. I knew how much work it took to run their farm and hoped that I could help.

"Well, the horses have been in the stall all winter and their manure needs to be shoveled out," Peter sighed, scratching his head, "But you probably don't want to do that."

"That would be great; show me what to do," I volunteered, looking forward to physical labor after months at my desk by a window that looked out at a brick wall.

---

[2] Peter Kane Default (1923-2013), American poet published in the *New Yorker*; Liberal Party Congressional candidate against the Vietnam War; subject of the documentary film: "What I Meant To Tell You: An American Poet's State of the Union," which premiered at the Berkshire International Film Festival in 2010.

Peter led me to the barn and, handed me a pitchfork, and joked, "Have fun." He opened the top of the door and slammed the bottom half to keep the horses in.

I began tossing the manure out through the opening. It was hard going, as the manure was heavier than I imagined. I now saw why he had postponed the chore. One of the horses turned to watch, seeming cheered that his living quarters were finally being cleaned.

Around mid-morning, as a load of manure flew into space—I was gone. All sense of self disappeared. There was no *me*—only blissful light and consciousness.

I don't know how long I was gone, but after a while I began to return. I was surprised to find myself gazing into space. I put the pitchfork down and walked outside. I stood in the sun breathing the clear country air. After a while Ruth rang the bell for lunch and I walked back to the house.

Next morning before breakfast, I went again to the barn to shovel manure—hoping for another experience of *satchitananda.* The horse turned in greeting as I picked up the pitchfork and went to work. For the next hour I flung manure out the window with great gusto, waiting again to dissolve into light, but nothing happened.

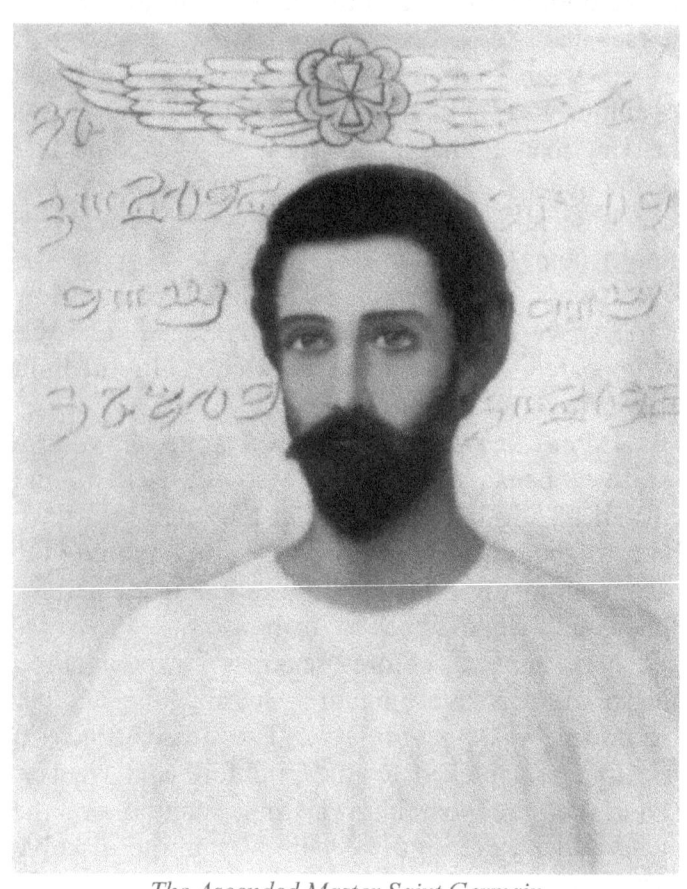

The Ascended Master Saint Germain

Disagreement With Saint Germain

The Masters almost never tell anyone what to do, which is how you can tell that most "channelings" come from imagination, not from an enlightened being. Mastery is only achieved through personal effort, not by sitting at the feet of a channel.[3]

However, the first time I consciously met Saint Germain etherically, he did tell me what to do and further, what was going to happen in the year ahead; but I didn't like anything he said. He told me that I would sell my idyllic hilltop farm near Woodstock; that I would return to India, where I had almost died; that I would move to Mount Shasta, which in 1972 was a logging town that regarded long-hairs with hostility; and lastly, he instructed me to change my last name to Mt. Shasta. I had not asked Neem Karoli Baba for a Hindu name like Ram Dass, Krishna Das, or Jai Gopal, so I certainly wasn't going to take a mountain for a name, and I told him so.

"You will," he asserted.

"No, I won't," I persisted.

"We shall see…," he concluded.

Of course he was right, and everything he said did come to pass. People pay a lot of money going to psychics and channelers to learn the future or find out what they should do, but those channelers would soon be out of business if they delivered messages

---

[3] Saint Germain told Pearl in the 1940s that channeling would become so prevalent as to greatly dilute spirituality in the West.

like the one Saint Germain gave. No one wants to be told they are going to fall in love and have their heart broken, that they are going to be fired from their job, or find out they have a serious illness. However, these are all common occurrences that are more likely to happen than winning the lottery and sailing off into the sunset with one's true love.

One time, Master Kuthumi appeared before me in physical form in the bus depot in Tel Aviv.[4] He emanated so much love I wanted to prostrate at his feet and ask him to accept me as his disciple. I begged inwardly for him to tell me why I was there and explain my future destiny; but all he said was, "Get on the next bus."

Many will say to me in that day, 'Lord, Lord, have we not prophesied in your name, cast out demons in your name, and done many wonders in your name?' And then I will declare to them, 'I never knew you; depart from me, you who practice iniquity.

Matthew 7:21-23

---

[4] This and other real-life contacts with Ascended Masters are described in greater detail in my book, *Apprentice to the Masters: Adventures of a Western Mystic, Book II.*

Holding the Field

An American *sadhu* (wandering yogi) by the name of Jonathan River Wolfe, spent every summer high up on the far side of Mount Shasta below the glacier. In the old days in India it was easy to be a s*adhu,* as they were held in high regard. People felt they accumulated good karma by feeding them and sadhus could stay overnight in the ubiquitous temples. In the West, however, many viewed these wandering mystics as lazy hippies. When I first came to Mount Shasta in 1972, signs hung in the doors of businesses on Main Street that said, "No hippies or longhairs allowed."

Jonathan grew up in a well to do home in Ohio, but he suffered under a domineering mother. At the age of fourteen, fortune chose him to be a foreign exchange student in India. As soon as he arrived, he felt at home. He realized he had been a *sadhu* in a past life and wanted to return to that path.

Like many of us born in the West who did not find materialism and ego-centered goals fulfilling, he sought a more spiritual life. When he returned from that year in India, he did not want to go to college as his parents had hoped, but to live in nature and meditate.

His parents gave him a hundred dollars every birthday, which was enough in those days to fly standby to the Hawaiian island of Kauai. He spent winters there in the jungle and in the spring would return to Mount Shasta. That is when I met him—in

Pearl's living room. It was like meeting a long-lost brother. Like many of the others who came to see Pearl, he wanted to connect with Saint Germain. To attain this goal, he used the tantric method Pearl had taught him:

Enter a state of meditation where the mind is still. Repeat the affirmation,

I am the Presence of the Ascended Master Saint Germain now manifest in my life and world.

Visualize the Master standing before you as a living, breathing being. Dissolve this visualization into a ball of amethyst light that merges into your heart center. You become Saint Germain—his heart is your heart—a ball of violet light. His mind is your mind--his body is your body—his violet aura is your aura. You radiate the amethyst light of forgiveness, transmutation, and freedom to humanity.

Lastly, dissolve the visualization. However, you can also imagine that he is hovering above your head—your I Am Presence still further above him.

One night after a group meditation at Pearl's house, during which the radiation of Saint Germain was particularly strong, Jonathan began walking home to his teepee that was in the trees not far off the road that led up the Mountain. As it was cold and there was snow on the ground, he walked quickly, thinking that he would make a pot of tea when he reached home.

Just as he arrived at the turn-off into the woods, a police car pulled up beside him and the window rolled down. "Hey, where are you going?" the officer asked.

"I'm going to my teepee," Jonathan replied with apprehension.

"Really, you live in a teepee?" the officer asked with curiosity, "Can I see it?"

"Sure, come on in and I'll make you some tea," Jonathan offered.

"OK, just let me park the car."

The policeman pulled off the road, shut off the engine, and followed in Jonathan's footsteps to the teepee. When they arrived, he parted the flap for the officer to enter. Inside, he offered him a seat on a trunk while he brewed the tea. When it was ready, Jonathan poured two mugs and they drank together. The officer commented appreciatively, "You've got quite a place here!"

Twenty minutes later, as he readied to leave, the officer said, "Is it OK if I come and visit again?"

"Sure, anytime," Jonathan replied, opening the flap.

Next morning, when Jonathan went to see Pearl and told her about the policeman's visit, she said, "Jonathan, do you really think a policeman is going to drink tea with you in your teepee at ten o'clock at night? Do you know who that was?"

"Saint Germain!" Jonathan exclaimed. You know, the moment he sat down I suspected something. I never saw this policeman in town and he had such beautiful energy."

"Exactly," Pearl said, with a twinkle in her eye.

A week later, Jonathan said the beautiful energy of that policeman still lingered in the teepee.

A few days later he hiked up the Mountain, crossed over the ridge and down into Squaw Meadow where Guy Ballard, author of *Unveiled Mysteries,* met Saint Germain during the summer of 1930. He set up camp there, which he called Shiva Camp, after the Hindu God who destroys illusion. People visited, often bringing him food. Sometimes they would spend the night. As the snow melted, he moved the camp higher, until by late summer it was just below the glacier. Much of the time he wandered around naked, bathing in the stream of glacial water, and meditating on a rock in the sun.

When he descended the mountain every couple of weeks and came into town, he sat outdoors at the Heart Rock Café, which was in the middle of town. He emanated so much Christ energy that people wanted to sit near him, and strangers often bought him breakfast. I used to see him there gazing up at the mountain, absorbed in contemplation.

On the 4th of July, the city streets were packed with people who came from all over Northern California and Southern Oregon to participate in the events the city sponsored. I was surprised to see Jonathan at the café, as I thought he would be shy of the crowds and remain in the solitude of the mountain. Yet here he was, surrounded by people, the loud speaker blaring instructions to those who wanted to participate in the annual races. He was remarkably peaceful, his blue eyes gazing at the crowd.

"I thought you would stay on the mountain, Jonathan?" I asked.

"No, I felt the need to be in town to do my work."

I was surprised at his use of the word, "work," for that was a subject he avoided, much to the annoyance of those who thought he should get a job.

"What work?" I asked, curious.

"Holding the field. That's my work…to hold the field."

I realized then that just by being present he could transmit the Christ frequency to all. Later I read that Krishna said:

> *Know the field, as well as the Knower*
> *of the field. I am the Self seated*
> *in the hearts of all beings.*
>
> -Krishna, *Bhagavad Gita*

I invited Jonathan out for breakfast one morning at the Black Bear Diner down by the freeway. He had bussed tables there for a few weeks when he first came to town. Back then it was called "Jerry's," but today the owner, Bob Manley, bought us breakfast.

He must have sensed Jonathan's energy, for whenever we ate there, he picked up the bill.

Remembering the old days at his last paying job, Jonathan laughed. One night he had been there at the beginning of a freak spring snow storm and Melissa, a good-hearted waitress, gave him the key to her nearby apartment so he could crash on her sofa.

Now he lived on grace, trusting he would be provided for—and he was. Although some people called him a freeloader, they would undoubtedly have said the same thing about Jesus.

One day we sat at a window table at the Black Bear. It looked out on Lake Street and the Safeway across the street. He confided that he was still suffering from the bite of a brown recluse spider that had bitten him while living in the jungle on Kauai. What helped the most, he said, was reciting the Vajrasattva mantra that had been given to him by a Tibetan Lama. When I asked to hear it, he chanted the Sanskrit words softly and I was immediately elevated in consciousness.

I asked him to teach it to me, but he said, "You are supposed to receive the empowerment from a Lama before you do the practice, but I will give you the words."

Seeing the Safeway sign across the street seemed to be a message from Divine Mind that it was safe to learn without a lama. So, he wrote the words and as I read them, I felt a shiver of bliss.

"Jonathan, I don't need permission from any Lama. I just received the empowerment direct from

Vajrasattva himself!" The vibration itself was the empowerment. Although the mantra contained one hundred syllables, miraculously I knew it by heart the next day. That mantra Jonathan taught me at the Black Bear Diner became a core practice for many years to come, and it never failed to raise me into a consciousness and purity beyond all human concerns.[5] As I recited it, I would visualize myself as the Deity and say,

I am Vajrasattva.

---

[5] Sanskrit mantras not only invoke a Deity, the mantra itself is the activity of the Deity. Hence, by reciting a mantra, reality is altered. Affirmations are somewhat different. An I Am affirmation recited in one's native language can also be effective if done with consciousness of the Source. Unfortunately, many people recite affirmations solely from the mind. As they get caught up in thought, they lose the connection with the Source and merely invoke their own personal will. For this reason, Sanskrit mantras are frequently used in Tibet and India. The Sanskrit alphabet is largely made up of primordial sounds that invoke aspects of universal consciousness. That is why babies all over the world make the same sounds regardless of their native language. Some of these sounds are the Sanskrit consonants: Mama, Dada, Papa, Kaka, Gaga. Some of the vowels are also sounds people make in certain universal situations: Ahh, Eee, Ooo, Ohh, Eh, I, Ow, and Umm.

Taking on Karma

In Hawaii Jonathan heard a Lama talk about compassion. He said we should have compassion for all beings, even those in the lower realms such as demons and hungry ghosts. These ghosts are people who die with unfulfilled cravings, hence "hungry," that prevent them from being reborn as humans until their obsessive desires are transmuted. Having compassion for these beings, Jonathan vowed to leave his body that night during sleep and go to the hungry ghost realm to help those imprisoned there.

He went to a land where he saw people suffering, and as he listened to their woeful complaints, the ruler of that world, Yamataka, appeared bearing a jeweled rod. "So, you want to help them?" he asked.

Jonathan nodded, and Yamataka smote his arm with the rod. When he woke in the morning the arm Yamataka had hit now trembled. He ignored it, but after a week of continued trembling he went back to the Lama and asked for help.

The Lama nodded without apparent sympathy and told him to continue reciting the mantra. The tremor increased over the years until eventually his whole body shook. It appeared to be Parkinson's disease, but doctors could not diagnose it as that. Despite his suffering, he felt his wish to help people in the underworld had been granted—that he had taken on some of their suffering—and that by continuing the mantra he was advancing their purification. He continued reciting the one hundred syllable mantra that invokes Vajrasattva, the God of Purity, who invokes the mindstreams of all the Buddhas.[6]

Despite this tremor, Jonathan remained happy and good natured, so much so that he even cheered up others. If you were in a bad mood and went to see him, you were sure to leave happy. You felt *if he can be happy, despite trembling all the time, I can also be happy.*

He had pictures of saints and yogis from all over the world on his walls and conversed with them as old friends. His room was filled with their presence. Over time he became more and more like them, radiating inner joy. Some people spontaneously knelt at his feet and asked his blessing when they came into his presence.

One day his longtime friend, Jude, dropped by to visit. She often cooked meals for him and checked on him daily. She knocked on the door but received no answer. Since he never locked the door, she went in. He was lying on the floor, a peaceful expression

---

[6] The One Hundred Syllable mantra invokes oneness with all qualities of Divine Mind. "Whatever manifestations of realms, palaces, and forms there are…they do not exist on a gross level. They are forms of *shunyata* (emptiness) endowed with all the supreme qualities. Therefore, they are known as possessing the aspect of being without self-nature. The minds of those buddhas are continually filled with the wisdom of unchanging non-dual bliss emptiness." -Dilgo Khyentse Rinpoche.

on his face. He no longer trembled—and was free at last to journey among the stars.

Jonathan River Wolfe

Flying

I read in the paper that Dee Thurmond was opening a flight school at the Weed Airport, about 10 miles north of Mount Shasta on land where Pearl and Jerry's ranch had been located many years before. I felt inner guidance to visit the new business and transmit a blessing in the manner Pearl had instructed. By turning my attention inward and using I AM affirmations and visualizations I could make my thoughts a reality.

While I was doing this, a tall, intense young man walked up and introduced himself as Erik Kampe, a former "Green Beret" who had served in Vietnam, and now the chief flight instructor here.

"Would you like to see one of the planes?" Erik asked.

I said I would, so we walked over to a nearby Cessna 150.

"Would you like to get in?"

"Sure, why not?" I replied, and I started to walk to the passenger side.

"No, get into the pilot's seat."

I climbed in and found the wheel resting in my lap, an array of dials and instruments before me.

"Turn the ignition key," he said with a grin.

As the engine roared to life, I found myself reliving a childhood fantasy of someday being a jet fighter pilot.

"Would you like to taxi the plane around a bit?" Erik continued in a matter of fact way.

I said I would, so he told me to use the pedals to control the direction of the nose wheel, and soon we were at the beginning of the runway. Then he said, "Push the throttle forward all the way and keep the nose wheel on that yellow line."

The engine roared with power and we surged down the runway. As the nose lifted off the ground, we were suddenly airborne. I looked at Erik in shock, and he grinned, "Fun, isn't it?"

Peering out the side window, I watched the airport shrink and finally disappear. We kept climbing, ascending over fields, barns, and streams, soaring into the clouds and then into the blue sky.

He had me level off, made a left, and there was the airport again. After two more turns I saw the runway dead ahead.

"Cut the power and pull this knob," he said.

"What would happen if I didn't pull that knob?"

"The engine would stall, and we'd be killed."

"OK, I'll pull the knob," I said, which later I discovered sent heat to the carburetor to prevent it from icing.

"Now, line up the nose with those lights on the side of the runway. That will guide us to set the correct angle of descent."

"Flare up!" he shouted, a few seconds before the wheels touched the runway. The nose lifted and settled back down as two wheels, then the nose wheel, hit the pavement. At the end of the runway I turned the plane around and headed back up the taxiway to the airport office.

"Cut the engine," he ordered.

I turned the ignition and suddenly it was silent. I was stunned; I had just flown a plane with no previous instruction. When I had awakened that morning, I had not had any idea that I would fly a plane that day. Such was the life of a student of Saint Germain. For three years, I never knew what might come next.

"Be here Saturday at ten a.m. for your next lesson," Erik said. As I looked at him in disbelief, he shrugged, "Hey, it is what it is."

Lost Over the Mountains

After three months of flying lessons, I had made my first long-distance solo flight. I felt cocky, that I was a seasoned pilot who could do anything. Then, one day Erik said, "Hop in…fly me to Fort Jones."

That was a small town in the valley on the other side of the mountains, twenty miles west of the airport as the crow flies. I knew exactly where the town was since I had friends there and knew it shouldn't take more than fifteen-minutes from takeoff to landing.

We climbed into the plane and were soon cruising a thousand feet above the highest peak. It was a beautiful day and I was confident at how well the flight was going until Erik asked, "Where are we?"

"We're about half way to Fort Jones."

"About half way? Show me exactly where we are on the chart," Erik demanded.

Pulling the folded-up chart from between the seats, I opened it and pointed to a spot about half way to Fort Jones and said, "We're somewhere near here."

"Somewhere? Where is somewhere?"

"Well, I don't know exactly."

"What course heading have you been flying?"

"I haven't been following one," I confessed.

"You're lost!"

"No, I'm not."

"If you don't know where you are, then you're lost! A pilot needs to be impeccable. I want you to find our position, calculate a heading, and fly us back to the Weed airport."

Chagrinned, I used the radio to take a bearing from the Montague VOR radio beacon and another from the Redding beacon, and drew lines. We were where the two lines crossed, so I drew a line from that spot back to the Weed Airport, which was a heading of ninety-eight degrees. I banked the plane into a turn and rolled out when the compass showed that heading, and soon we were back where we had started.

"There are old pilots and there are bold pilots, but there are no old, bold pilots," Erik said, then stiffly walked away.

Although I always listened to intuition, from then on I flew by the book. On one occasion when the weather clouded over and I needed to find an emergency place to land, what Erik taught me saved my life.

Erik should have followed his own advice on impeccability. Next year he got a job as a pilot for FedEx and the tower cleared him to land behind a heavy commercial jet. He should have requested to go around and wait for the wake turbulence to clear, but he was in a hurry to complete the delivery and tried to land. The air turbulence was still active and flipped the plane upside down. Both Erik and the co-pilot were killed.

Flying by Intuition

God is My Co-Pilot was a book and later a film based on the experiences of Robert L. Scott during the Second World War. However, I always considered God as my pilot, myself as the co-pilot. After my experience with Erik, I always plotted my course carefully before take-off.

However, one day I took off in my Cessna and climbed to ten-thousand feet, almost the ceiling for this small-engine plane. I had no clear objective this day except to fly around the valley. It felt good just to get up there above human thoughts and emotions. Being up there was like meditation, where the only mind is your own. When I got up to that altitude all problems with other people disappeared. I could see what thoughts were mine and what thoughts came from others. All situations were revealed in a new light. On a commercial flight that doesn't work because you're surrounded by others and their problems.

I felt I was meant to go somewhere, but where? I invoked guidance with the affirmation,

I am going where I am meant to go, doing what I am meant to do.

I trimmed the plane so it would fly straight and level and set up a standard rate turn. I closed my eyes, knowing I would sense when headed in the direction I was meant to fly. I thought, *Erik would turn over in his grave if he saw me flying in circles at over a hundred miles an hour with my eyes closed!*

I heard, *turn out!* When I opened my eyes, the compass showed a heading of one hundred eighty-two degrees. *Hold this heading,* I heard. So, I continued for a few hours until I approached the San Francisco Bay area. I was running low on gas and wondered, *where to now?* I asked my Higher Self and the Ascended Masters but received no response. There were a lot of other planes near mine now, so I kept a sharp lookout.

Land now! I heard.

Looking down, I saw Novato ahead, and by the freeway was the Marin County Airport. After scanning for other traffic, I set up a glide and entered the airport landing pattern. Soon I was on the ground, taxiing up to the fence. I tied the plane down and walked up to the gate, wondering *why did the Masters send me here?*

"Peter! What are you doing here?" a man standing against the gate shouted. As I approached, he said, "Remember me? We met in Mount Shasta a few years ago. My wife and I were just talking about inviting you down to give a talk to our meditation group on the I AM teachings!"

"How did you know I was coming?"

"I was on my way home from work on the 101 Freeway and heard an inner voice say, 'Take the next exit and go to the airport,' and here I am. Will you come home and spend the night with us? My wife will be overjoyed. She'll call our friends and you can talk to us about the Masters."

As we left in his car, I saw a sign on the fence identifying this airport as Gnoss Field—which sounded like *gnosis,* the Greek word meaning spiritual knowledge and self-mastery.

Protected by Saint Germain

Whenever I flew, I asked Saint Germain to be the pilot and guide and direct my flight. Before I took off, I would say silently,

I am the Invincible Tube of Light about this plane. I am guided, directed, and protected by the Ascended Master Saint Germain.

Taking off one day, I heard a familiar voice on the radio, "Peter, turn left immediately! There is a plane headed your way."

I thought, *that's strange, ground control radio operators do not call by name for they don't even know your name—so they always call by the make and registration number of the plane. He should have addressed me, not as Peter, but as "Cessna two-two-eight-one-niner...."*

I recognized the voice, however—it was a friend who took flying lessons at the airport—so, I banked into a sharp left turn and was shocked as a large helicopter whizzed past, landing against the traffic pattern. It was illegal, but this was a remote area with almost no traffic, and he had taken a chance.

A few days later, I saw the friend whose voice I had had heard on the radio and thanked him for saving my life.

"What are you talking about? I haven't been to the airport in weeks."

I knew then, on that day the radio operator, as well as the pilot, had been Saint Germain.

Overcoming Shyness

During the time I was learning to fly, I hung out at the Weed airport. The flight school office was an old mobile home with a desk and a couple of sofas facing each other. All sorts of people gathered there, farmers, highway patrolmen, real estate agents; the desire to fly was the bond that brought us together.

Since everyone had different backgrounds, they had varying views. However, people tried not to irritate each other, and sought common ground—which frequently involved the weather. As a kid I had always been puzzled how adults would talk about what they thought the weather was going to do, but now I saw it had a purpose. Everyone felt good about having their say without being judged or criticized. On a clear day you could say, "I think it's going to cloud up this afternoon," or if it was raining you could say "The sun is going to come out soon." People's opinions were respected, so everyone felt good.

As a kid I had been shy, afraid to speak up; but now I began to express myself. I told the Highway Patrolman sitting on the sofa across from me, "It's going to be warm and sunny tomorrow," and he said, "You know, you could be right."

But then, the farmer standing in the corner said, "No, my cows are acting strange, which means it's going to rain." Nobody was wrong, and everyone felt accepted. Through hours of conversation in that airport office, I learned to find the common ground.

After a while I could talk with anyone. I was amazed that beneath the various, sometimes rough, exteriors, everyone was basically good. This was what Pearl called objective teaching. The Masters could not have taught this in their retreat inside the Mountain, but only in daily life.

Skydiving

I meditated on my I AM Presence every day, as well as Its oneness with the Ascended Masters whose pictures adorned my walls. At night before bed, I read from the *I AM Discourses* (Saint Germain Foundation), and prayed that during my sleep I would receive guidance for the following day, and started the next day with the affirmation,

I am the Great Divine Director of this day.

Then I would try to follow the promptings of my heart throughout the day, no matter how unusual or unpredictable the guidance might seem.

While free of my denser body at night, I was often conscious of working with the Ascended Masters. I would go to their retreats at various locations around the world and work with other souls who were also students of the Masters, seeking ways to increase the consciousness of humanity. These experiences were often so vivid it was difficult to concentrate on my work in my real estate office during the day. I often wondered how much longer I had to stay in physical embodiment and when my ascension would be completed. The more I meditated the more my vibratory frequency increased, and the less connected I felt to Earth.

One day I was sent by the Masters to do work for them in New York City. This involved going to various locations around the city and invoking pillars of light they intended to sustain. I also invoked the Violet Consuming Flame to purify the City, and Archangel Michael to remove discarnate entities. Wherever I went, I turned my attention to the inner sun, sending forth rays of light. As the light blazed forth, I became more and more luminous. My *atman,* known in the West as the I AM Presence, became a tangible force working in harmony with the Ascended Masters, Angels, and Cosmic Beings— who all poured forth their own radiation.

At night when the work was done, I took the train from Grand Central Station back to the suburbs, where I was staying with my mother. After dinner one night she turned on the TV and we saw a program on skydiving. As I watched people jump from the plane and soar back to earth, Saint Germain said, to my great surprise, "I want you to do the same."

Since I was a pilot and had spent a lot of time aloft, skydiving did not attract me. However, it occurred to me, *perhaps this is the means the Masters are providing to leave my body?*

Next day I looked for skydiving schools but there were none nearby, so I forgot about it. *Perhaps I had been mistaken?* I had learned, when the Masters wanted me to do something, they always provided the means. If the means did not appear, then I was mistaken in tuning in.

My work in New York was finished, and I bought a plane ticket to fly from New York to Los

Angeles. There I would switch to a flight to Redding, sixty miles from Mount Shasta.

Checking in at LaGuardia airport, I found the plane was going to be only half full, so I asked for a seat in the wide center row, hoping I would be able to lie down and take a nap. But the agent said there was another person in my row, and changing seats was not an option.

As I walked down the aisle to my assigned seat, I was shocked to see the woman occupying the adjacent seat wearing a jump suit like the skydivers.

"Do you skydive?" I blurted.

"Why yes, I do," she replied. "If you are continuing on this flight to Hawaii, I'll give you the phone number of my instructor there."

Continue on to Hawaii...go skydiving? It was another setup by the Masters. Here now was the means to do what Saint Germain had asked. When the plane landed, I went to the airline desk and changed the ticket. Now I was going to Honolulu.

Miraculously, there was a single room at the famous Halekulani Hotel on the beach at Waikiki. Despite it being the busy season, they gave me the room at a reduced price——which seemed another indication I was following the Master's Plan.

As soon as I reached my room, I called the owner of the skydiving school, Byron Black, and he said he would pick me up at nine a.m. the next morning. He was right on time and I climbed in the car with a few others who were going to make the jump. We headed toward Haleiwa and in about an hour we pulled off the road in front of a single engine plane at the end of a dirt strip.

We climbed out of the car and Byron's son had us sign legal statements saying we realized the danger in jumping out of a plane and released them from liability—not an encouraging way to begin. However, soon the instruction began, and he showed us how to release the main chute if it didn't open and to deploy the reserve chute. There was a small radio transceiver attached to our chests that could be used to call for help, but I wondered what kind of help you could get hurtling toward the ground at 200 miles per hour?

As practice, we took turns climbing onto a platform about seven feet high and jumping off, which was supposed to simulate the impact of hitting the ground. The person next to me whispered in my ear that in the army the paratroopers train for two weeks before the first jump; however, Byron assured us we were ready. He handed out the chutes and we suited up. Soon, I was climbing into the plane with the instructor and another jumper.

I looked at my chute and wondered who had packed it and if he had been paying attention. *Was it going to open?* The chute's rip-cord was attached to a static line, a cord tied to a bolt inside the plane, that was supposed to deploy the chute after you jumped. I wondered, *if the shoot opens so reliably, why do they spend so much time teaching you what to do if it doesn't open?*

The small plane hurtled down the runway. Being a pilot myself, I watched with interest as we strove to gain altitude, climbing above the sugarcane fields, swinging out over the ocean, and then back over the fields to our jump location.

"Whatever you do, don't land in the ocean," the instructor shouted over the roar of the engine. I wondered how that was to be avoided if the wind picked up, but it was too late to ask. He shouted, "Prepare to jump!"

We seemed awfully close to the ground, and I asked the instructor, "Can't we go up another few thousand feet so we will have more time to deploy the reserve chute if something goes wrong?"

"We always do the first jump from three thousand feet," he snapped back. *Yeah, to save money on gas*, I thought.

"First jumper!" the instructor shouted. The other jumper climbed out on the two-by-four that served as a step bolted to the side of the plane. His hands clenched the strut.

"Jump!" the instructor shouted.

The man threw his arms back as instructed and a second later his chute blossomed into a beautiful white canopy.

As I readied myself, I saw an orange glow at the back of the plane that assumed the unmistakable form of Sathya Sai Baba. His presence was reassuring, even more so when he raised his hands in a blessing and said, "Have no fear, I am here."

Does this mean he's going to protect me, or that I am about to crash and leave my body? I wondered. But there was no time for thought.

"You're next! Climb out, hands on the strut," the instructor shouted.

I moved from the back of the plane where I was crouched, to the front, right side, where the door had been removed to leave a gaping hole through which the wind roared. Looking down, my heart rose in my throat. I could see the other jumpers as a small cluster on the ground looking up at us. The cars they had arrived in looked like toys. Overcoming the initial shock, I placed one foot on the wood step and gripped the strut with both hands.

"Jump!" the instructor shouted.

I threw my arms upward into the air and arched backward. I waited for the jerk of the chute, but felt nothing, only the wind whistling in my ears. *Where is my chute?"* It was not open.

Instead of a white canopy I was supposed to see overhead, there was ragged fabric spinning around and around. Time stopped. I struggled to pull myself up on the shrouds, then let go in the hope of snapping the chute open, but nothing happened. I was too busy to feel fear as I tried again and again, but the chute continued to spiral overhead. *So, this is it!* I thought.

I saw the ground looming and realized it was too late to deploy the reserve chute. Time had run out; my life was over—everything went dark.

I was sitting at a table with three Masters in white robes. In the center was Saint Germain, and he said with a smile, "Peter, you still have much to accomplish on Earth. Here, have an ice-cold beer!"

"What!" I exclaimed, but he and the other Masters were gone. I found myself lying on the ground, gasping for air, pains shooting through my feet.

"Here, have an ice-cold beer!" someone said, thrusting an ice cold bottle into my hand. I raised my head and saw that I was holding a beer. What was this? I had not had alcohol for twenty years, yet Saint Germain had just offered me a beer and here it was!

"Are you OK?" the instructor beside me shouted?

I said I was, but hot needles pierced my toes and pains shot up my legs.

"Drink…it will bring you in your body," the instructor insisted.

I took a few long swigs from the frosty bottle and felt a bit better. Two men carried me back to the staging area where one said, "Here, have another," and thrust a second bottle into my hand.

"Tough luck, kid…you probably broke a few toes…but, sometimes that's the way it is."

The Flying Immortals

There were Masters in ancient China who supposedly lived hundreds of years and could fly in their physical bodies. I had seen martial arts films portraying such beings soaring among the tree tops. I wanted to believe in them but being a Westerner with a scientific background, I didn't believe without proof. Then, when I read Ron Teeguarden's book, *Chinese Tonic Herbs* (Japan Publications, 1985), in which he interviewed someone who claimed to have first-hand knowledge of these beings known as flying immortals, I began to entertain the possibility that such beings had existed. Ancient Chinese art and literature certainly make reference to these Masters.

I used to have a farm on a hilltop near Woodstock, New York, where in 1968 I tried to start an ashram. People used to come and visit from all over, some staying overnight, others stayed months. One of these people who visited was a healer named, Sarada. I had recently returned from a six month pilgrimage in India, where I had developed serious health problems, and she was happy to do healing work. Her specialty was channeling energy through her hands from her Higher Self. Her hands never touched my body but focused energy to the areas that needed healing.

One night, after working all day in the garden, I was exhausted and lay face down on my thin futon that lay stretched on the wood floor boards of the old farmhouse. When Sarada offered energy work, I gratefully accepted. The session began normally, with her hands about a foot above my back. Then, she had me turn over so she could work on my digestion. The energy was so relaxing I dozed off and she went to her room to read a book.

Eventually, I awakened but I could no longer feel the floor. I turned and saw the top of a trunk a few feet away. *That's strange,* I thought, when I lay down I saw the side of the trunk—now I am looking down on the top.

When I realized I was floating a couple of feet in the air, I tried to sit up, but crashed to the floor.

"What happened?" Sarada said, rushing in.

"I was levitating!"

"You must have been, because the whole floor shook," Sarada said. "I have heard of it happening to other people too, but I have never had it happen to one of my clients."

I began taking the legends of the flying immortals more seriously after that. It took another forty-five years before I discovered how levitation could be accomplished consciously.

Identified Flying Object

I met a former military officer by the name of Wendelle Stevens in Mount Shasta in 1974. He used to photograph UFO phenomena in the Arctic for the air force. When he retired, he continued on his own to investigate cases where there was suspected extraterrestrial contact. His work was highly respected because he did not jump to conclusions but applied military discipline to his investigations. Shortly after I met him, he went to Switzerland to look into the Billie Meier case. Years later I found myself living in Tucson, Arizona, where Wendelle lived also, and I went to visit him.

He told me that Eduard "Billie" Meier claimed to have been contacted by a woman from the Pleiades, who met with him on numerous occasions and even took him on board her space craft. There were many claims of fraud, but Wendelle kept an open mind. He had become a trusted friend of the Meier family and one day as they were sitting around the kitchen table, Billie straightened up and announced, "They're signaling me that I'm going to have a contact."

Although a hard rain had begun to fall, he rose and headed for the screen door. Wendelle followed one step behind. Billie stepped outside and the door slammed. A split second later Wendelle opened the door, but Billie had disappeared. There was only a single footstep in the mud. An hour later Billie phoned from a village ten kilometers away. When Wendelle picked him up, Billie's clothes were still dry despite the rain.

Mother Mary and her Immaculate Heart.

The Power of Purity

In India in the 70s most of the homes in rural villages had no running water or bathrooms. Every morning your neighbors would go out in the field and relieve themselves without a care in the world. If you grew up in that culture, it was as natural for you as it was for the family dog.

In the old days in this tropical climate, women often went bare-chested like men, and women nursed their babies in public without a care. However, when the British invaded India they imposed their Victorian ideas of modesty, and now women were not supposed to bare an arm above the elbow or a leg above the knee. Under this onerous burden, and without baths, I wondered how people managed to wash themselves.

That question was answered one day as I went to buy fresh mangos. I walked down a path through a field until I arrived at a village of a dozen thatched huts centered around a well. A pump offered water from a spigot, and as I walked toward it to cool myself off, I noticed a young woman beginning to bathe beside the well.

She placed an extra sari on the wall behind the pump, then washed one part of her body at a time, never revealing more than the outer segment of each limb. No one paid any attention to her as she seemed enveloped in an aura of purity.

By the end of her ablutions she had completely washed, cleaned the old sari, and wore a fresh one.

Even though I had watched the whole procedure, I could not understand how she had accomplished this. She seemed unaware of my presence.

How different this was from many bikini clad women on the beach at Santa Monica, eager to attract male attention. Both eastern and western cultures handled that sacred energy so differently.

Thinking back on the woman at the well, I realized that her washing had been a conscious ritual in which she visualized herself as the Deity while reciting the mantra for purity. Employing that tantric ritual, she was not just a woman taking a bath, but a Goddess purifying the world.

I saw that aura of purity invoked in other circumstances as well, such as protection against disease. My first guru, Ramamurti Mishra, was a medical doctor who volunteered to go to Bangladesh to help during a cholera epidemic. People asked him if he was afraid of getting sick, but he just smiled. After two months living and working in villages of the sick and dying, he returned in perfect health.

Baba Visits in a BMW

While visiting Sathya Sai Baba in Puttaparthi, India, in 1972, he made it clear I should meditate on "I Am."[7] I soon discovered that to accomplish this I first had to meditate on *who am "I?"*

Almost forty years later, in the fall of 2010, I was meditating in my shrine room in Mount Shasta, when I felt Baba's unmistakable presence. His love filled the room as he said, "I am going around the world asking my devotees for permission to leave my body."

Running the ashram and granting interviews consumed most of his day, and I knew that without these burdens he would have more freedom to travel the world in his higher body and help those who truly needed him.

"Of course, Baba, it's alright with me. I understand and will try to let go of my attachment to your physical form."

He nodded in acknowledgment and said, "Come visit me and I will give you an interview before I leave my body." Despite weeks spent sleeping

---

[7] This experience is recorded in my autobiographical, *Search for the Guru: Adventures of a Western Mystic, Book I.* Subsequent experiences with the Ascended Masters, particularly with Saint Germain, are recorded in, *Apprentice to the Masters: Adventures of a Western Mystic, Book II* (Church of the Seven Rays, publisher of both volumes).

outside his door, he had never granted me a private audience, though he often came in dreams.

I arrived in Puttaparthi for Naviratri, a nine-day celebration of various forms of the Goddess, but the ashram was crowded with tens of thousands of people, all wanting contact with him. I didn't see how I would get an interview. As I sat in the darshan hall, shoulder to shoulder with thousands of enthusiastic devotees, the situation seemed hopeless. When Baba finally appeared, it was as an orange blur far in the front of the hall. I thought, *there is no way he will single me out of this crowd.*

The love flowing from the crowd toward him was overwhelming. As they began chanting "Sai Ram…Sai Ram…Sai Ram," the love that filled the hall was overwhelming. I felt my heart breaking and I began to cry.

I lowered my head to hide the tears running down my cheeks and was suddenly lifted out of my body. I found myself sitting at Baba's feet, his orange robe before me and I placed my forehead on his knee. I felt his hand come down on my head. With utter sweetness, he said "My son, you have my eternal blessings…I will be with you always."

For a moment I sobbed uncontrollably, not wanting to ever leave his presence, but soon I was back among the crowd.

I returned to Mount Shasta, and five months later, on Easter day, 2011, Sai Baba departed his physical body as he had said. Although I had accepted his departure theoretically, my heart longed now to feel he was still present on earth in human form.

Although he had said he would always be with me, I began to doubt and longed for some sign from him that he was still with me. Then, one day I heard him say, "Go for a walk, my boy."

Was I imagining his voice out of desire for contact with him? Regardless, I walked out the door and ambled down the street as the voice had directed. Since I lived in a small housing development with almost no traffic, I walked down the center of the road. As I turned down Mountain View Avenue, a black BMW Roadster Z4 sports car with the top down rounded the corner from the main street, Mount Shasta Boulevard, and headed toward me.

It was identical to the one I had admired months before on a stopover in Switzerland on the way back from India. Walking down the street with my friend, Ruth, I saw it parked outside a bank. Joking, I said to Ruth, "Even though I don't like black, I would be happy if you gave me a car like this for Christmas!"

An identical black BMW now came toward me, and none other than Sathya Sai Baba was behind the wheel; but he appeared about thirty-five with radiant, black hair, and instead of his usual orange robe he sported a black leather jacket and black-rimmed sunglasses. Strangely, the car did not make a sound other than that of the tires rolling on the asphalt. I was so shocked I did not move out of the road, and the BMW passed a foot from my leg. As he cruised past, Baba flashed a dazzling smile and raised his hand in the familiar *abhaya* gesture, meaning "Have no fear, I am here."

Transfixed, I turned to see where he drove. As the car receded, I noticed no fumes came from the tailpipe.

Who can he be visiting? I wondered, as I knew none of the neighbors were devotees of his. I turned and followed back up the road to see where he went. As the road was a dead end, I knew he could not leave without passing me again. This time I would stop him. Yet when I rounded the bend, the street was empty. Baba and his black BMW had disappeared. I heard his voice then within me, "Didn't I tell you, I am with you always?"

The Masters Save Me Again

I wrote the second part of my autobiography, *Apprentice to the Masters: Adventures of a Western Mystic, Book II,* before I wrote the first part, *Search for the Guru,* as I felt those more recent experiences with the Ascended Masters were more unique than the first part of my life where, like many others in the 70s, I was awakening spiritually. When I began editing the manuscript of my adventures with Saint Germain, El Morya, Kuthumi, and other Ascended Masters, I was a guest at the home of Jiddu Krishnamurti in Ojai. He had long since passed on, but I thought it ironic that after a lifetime of him telling people to ignore the Masters and all other gurus, I would be assembling a book about them in his house.

This was a book that had been written episode by episode over the course of about thirty-five years, beginning in nineteen seventy-four, a year after I met Pearl. When I told a visitor an experience with a Master, they would say "You should write that down," and so I did, not expecting it would end up in a book. Finally, I sent some of these manuscripts to a professional editor to see if they merited publication. She was enthusiastic so I went ahead; and the editing of that book progressed rapidly.

However, when I decided to write about the first part of my life, I ran into all kinds of obstacles. The more I wrote about my childhood in New York, and my time in the City in the late sixties, the more things

I remembered that I wanted to write about: my experiences with Alan Ginsburg; Jack Kerouac's girlfriend, Dody Muller, at whose loft I used to crash; and the Hare Krishna devotees who chanted in Tompkins Square within earshot of my window.

One day, feeling anxious and frustrated, I put my finger on the Delete button. I felt *I'm wasting my time on this book no one will want to read anyway!*

At the last minute, I decided to pause the deletion and go up the Mountain to ask the Maha Chohan what to do. I parked near where I knew his temple to be and began trudging uphill through the snow. I had not quite reached the sacred location when I heard him say, *"You are getting bogged down in the New York scene. Omit the last ten pages and start writing about your spiritual adventures in India."*

I was stunned at such good editorial advice, but it was not what I wanted to hear. I wanted permission to quit writing entirely, as remembering and writing about my early life was a painstaking process. Shaking my head in annoyance, I continued hiking uphill thinking *I've had enough! I'm going to go as far up the Mountain as I can, lie down in the snow, and fall asleep.*

"Peter, turn around!" the Maha Chohan said, but I kept walking.

"I said, turn around," he repeated.

"Oh yeah, why?" I asked, belligerently, still frustrated with my writing.

"Because, I have sent people to see you, and they are waiting," he answered.

"I don't see anyone," I said, glancing back over my shoulder.

"They will be here shortly, now turn around and go back to the parking lot."

Grudgingly, I turned around thinking, *I will check it out, but if no one is there I am going back up the mountain.* I would never have been so contrary if he had appeared physically, but since I heard only an inner voice I wondered if it was really him. Or, was it my own mind?

Reaching the parking lot, I discovered a crowd of Indians. "Peter! I've been trying to reach you," a man said, holding his hands together in a prayerful greeting.

I remembered now that this man was Madhu, who had indeed sent both email and text messages requesting me to talk to the group he was bringing, but I had been so immersed in writing I had ignored the messages. Now, here they were, all one hundred-fifty of them. "Please, let us meditate with you," he begged.

Next thing, two people were at my feet, removing my boots, as the group gathered in a circle on the ground. They began chanting, then fell into meditation. After a while they opened their eyes and their leader invited me to talk to the group that night at the Mount Shasta Resort. My doubts about the wisdom of the Maha Chohan had been removed. Next day I followed his editorial advice and from then on, the writing went smoothly to the end of the book.

However, I had one more problem that almost caused me to delete the book from my computer. The book was finished, but I had many detailed footnotes the publisher wanted converted to endnotes. I found that Microsoft Word provided a way to do this automatically, so I converted them all in a second; but the next day I decided to use a different publisher who would allow the footnotes to remain, which I preferred for ease of reading. But I ran into a problem. The endnotes would not covert back, and the entire last section of the book froze. I could not change anything. I worked late into the night, searching online for ways to unlock Word, but to no avail. Once again, I thought *that's it, this is a sign I should not publish this book.*

I looked at the picture of Saint Germain that hung on the wall over my desk and thought, "Well, Saint Germain, if you want me to publish this book, you're going to have to do something because I've done all I can." Then, I went to bed.

In the morning as I lay in bed, I heard Saint Germain say, "Turn on your computer."

No way! I thought. The Word document had become so corrupted that even the thought of looking at it again repulsed me, but I heard the Master say again, "Peter, turn on your computer."

Okay, okay, I'll turn it on, but then I'm going to delete the book. I climbed out of bed and stumbled over to the desk and flipped the on-switch. It was an old computer and it took a while to boot up. Finally, there was the book on the screen. I scrolled to the end to look at the corrupted endnotes, but to my dismay they were not longer there. Scanning back through the book, I found that the footnotes had reappeared in the correct locations, and the document had become unfrozen. Bewildered, I looked up at the picture of Saint Germain that hung on the wall overlooking the desk.

"Saint Germain, did you do this?"

His image came to life, and I was shocked to see him wink. With a slight laugh, he said "Hey, I know Word."

Master Yu Tianjan

Ascension of Master Huiling

Saint Germain had sent me to Mount Shasta in 1973 to learn from Pearl how to bring the I Am Consciousness into daily life. After she died in 1990, I felt a certain emptiness; but when I ran into a student of Saint Germain by the name of Tahira, and she told me about an exceptional Chinese teacher in Los Angeles by the name of Yu Tianjian, known in the West as Master Yu (pronounced "you"), I was excited to meet him. He was recognized in China as a living Buddha, the 49th lineage holder of the Hanmi lineage that taught the esoteric Buddhist teachings that had been brought from India to China in the 8th century. He was recognized as a tulku soon after birth by a delegation of Buddhist monks who showed up unexpectedly at his family's home. As a boy he refused to follow the Dharma and instead joined the Communist Party. He rose in rank and was eventually appointed to run a large factory. Yet, inwardly, he was receiving spiritual teachings from an enlightened mahasiddha, Huiling, whose whereabouts were unknown. One day Huiling showed up at his factory and said, "Quit your job and come with me."

Without a moment's hesitation, Yu Tianjian sat down at his desk and wrote two letters of resignation, one from his job and the other from the Communist Party. Together, they left the factory and began walking around China. They eventually stayed in a Buddhist monastery where Huiling gave him intensive training. After six months, Huiling turned his sacred books over to Master Yu and said, "Follow me."

They left the monastery and walked into the desolate mountains. When he found the right spot, he taught Yu Tianjian two new mantras. Then he said, "I have brought you here to witness something few have ever seen. Walk away from me reciting the first mantra for the distance of one hundred paces, then sit down and close your eyes. You will hear something; then open your eyes, stand up, and walk back reciting the second mantra until you again reach this spot."

Yu Tianjin did as he was told, walking away, reciting the mantra for one hundred paces, and then sitting down. When he heard a whooshing sound, he opened his eyes and saw the sky successively illuminated by the colors of the rainbow, one wave of color after another. Knowing this was the sign, he rose and turned around, but Huiling was gone. Reciting the second mantra, he walked back to the original spot, but all that remained of his teacher were his robe, hair, and nails.

Adventures of Master Yu

Master Yu, as his followers called him, wandered around China for many years, giving the sacred teachings entrusted to him. However, the large following he attracted angered the Communists. They tried to eradicate anything spiritual, and many times he had to run for his life. In those days, the Red Guard executed many people simply for being among the upper classes or intelligencia. He said he was killed many times, but each time he revived. He showed a number of knife wounds to make his point.

One death was at the hands of his wife, who poisoned him when she learned he had donated all his money to various Buddhist monasteries rather than give it to her. His body was taken to the morgue and placed in a refrigerator pending identification. When his wife showed up to identify the body and the attendant pulled it out of the refrigerator, he sat up. His wife screamed and the attending doctor dropped dead of heart attack. After regenerating himself, Master Yu went to the mountains, but he always shunned cold after that. He continued to teach and heal and acquired over a million followers.

When I took initiation from him at his temple in East Los Angeles, I walked up an aisle between two opposing rows of his disciples, all wearing maroon robes, until I stood before a shrine on which seven bronze, life-size Buddhas reposed in meditation. Like most Americans, I was not used to bowing, for

America was founded on the principle of rebellion against tyrants. However, as I walked forward, my inner vision opened and I saw that no longer were those seated on either side Master Yu's disciples, but Ascended Masters of the Council of Light—and I fell to my knees. As I rose, a ray of light from each of the seven Buddhas entered my forehead and Master Yu beckoned me forward. Placing his hand on my head, he recited a Sanskrit mantra that sent a vibrant charge through my entire being. As I rose, I was ushered to a seat and handed a maroon robe and mala of large rudraksha beads.

When I asked later what the ceremony meant, I was told, "You just accepted Master Yu as your guru." Little did I realize all that would entail, for in most Asian cultures when you accept, and are accepted by a guru, you are expected to give total obedience. I wondered, *how is this total obedience thing going to work with the Woodstock generation, of which I am a part, that is used to doing their own thing?*

Master Yu gave me a book full of Sanskrit mantras, some of which were a page long, and told me to memorize them. Stunned at the enormity of this task, I left the temple and headed for the ocean. I felt it might be easier to learn the mantras amidst the sea breeze, away from the turmoil of the city.

I pulled into a parking space at Venice Beach, facing the ocean. I began chanting the first page-long mantra and suddenly entered a world beyond time and space. Before I realized, the sun was setting in the ocean. I knew I was expected back at the temple for the evening service, so I started back on the I-10 freeway.

Master Yu invoked the Medicine Buddha, as the evening service was dedicated to healing. This was his personal practice that involved his transformation into the Buddha of healing, a being made of lapis colored light that emitted rays of healing wherever needed. I had also learned this practice years before, but had never tried to actually heal anyone with it. However, that night I saw him work what would be called miracles. Person after person was cured, some scheduled to enter the hospital for surgery the next day. One woman had been deaf for ten years and was again able to hear.

After the service, we went outside. Most students left, but I remained, looking up at the night sky. Master Yu came up behind me and said, "Peter, tell me something, in China when I heal someone of cancer, they are grateful and want to give me something. On my last trip to China I healed a man dying of cancer. The doctors said he had a month to live. After he was healed, he gave me $40,000, his life savings. Tonight, the man I healed of cancer just gave $20. It seems people here don't feel grateful. Why is that?"

After a moment's thought, I replied, "I think it's because people feel that because the healing comes from God they don't have to pay."

"Yes, the healing does come from God, but the one who is the instrument of God has to live," Master Yu sighed, then walked back into the temple.

Master Yu and Peter Mt. Shasta at his home in Mount Shasta.

I got to know Master Yu very well. One night he invited me to his house for dinner, which I realized was a great honor. He was married to a beautiful, powerful Chinese business woman who cooked a sumptuous feast. He sat at the head of the table and seated me at his right hand. Encouraging me to sample all the delicacies, I plunged my chopsticks into a bowl of special noodles just as he put his chopsticks in the dish also. For a moment, we looked into each other's eyes, and the recognition of a deep bond passed between us. He nodded significantly and poured me a glass of Chinese Vodka. Although I protested that I did not drink hard liquor, he insisted I join him in a toast to the spread of the Buddha

Dharma, and his teachings in particular. Little did I realize that he intended for me to play a part in the propagation of that Dharma as his spiritual heir.

A month later he came to Mount Shasta to give a talk at the city park. The day before the talk he came to my house for dinner. While waiting for the meal to be served, the woman who had cooked the meal confided that she was having a gall stone attack and suffering severe pain. She wanted to know if Master Yu would heal her or if she should go to the hospital.

I asked him and he smiled, then told the woman to sit and close her eyes. He did not touch her but allowed her to remain on the other side of the room while he continued to tell jokes to our group of a dozen dinner guests. After five minutes, he asked her, "What are you feeling?"

"It feels like a giant hand is squeezing my gall bladder and crushing the stones."

A few minutes later he told her to open her eyes. She stood up, completely free of pain, and during the following year she never had any problems with her gall bladder. In fact, her overall health improved greatly. The next night, during his talk at the city park, he was no longer the charming entertainer he had been at dinner, but seemed transformed into a living Buddha. In all my years seeking wisdom, I never heard anyone talk so clearly about the nature of mind. He was truly inspiring, and the audience was enthralled. Afterward, many people asked to study with him.

The next day, his translator phoned and asked me to come to the house they were renting, as the Master had something important to discuss. I was escorted into a back room where I was alone with Master Yu and his translator. I sensed something of importance was about to unfold. I was right, as Master Yu explained he wanted me to be his dharma heir. He felt that in New Age America I was ideally suited to transmit his teachings. He said I would travel with him and receive half the financial proceeds. I was shocked at the honor and generosity of his offer.

"Is there any reason you cannot accept?" he asked.

"Well, you should know that although I have been studying with you for the past year, I am also a student of the Master Saint Germain, who is my primary teacher."

The translator gagged and hid his face in his hands. In China to say such a thing would be considered a grave insult. However, Master Yu seemed undisturbed and continued, "That's perfectly alright, but from now on you will receive all your instructions from Saint Germain through me. Do you understand?"

"I am sorry, Master Yu, but that is not acceptable. I get my guidance from my own Higher Self or directly from Saint Germain and do not need any intermediary; but thank you for your offer."

Master Yu's face turned red and I felt a wave of anger arise in him, so I bowed and walked out. As I left the house someone walking up the path asked, "Is Master Yu here?"

"He is," I said, and at that moment I realized the lesson. The name, Master Yu, means *you are the Master.*

I walked down the path feeling a weight had been lifted, knowing that never again would I entertain the thought I needed someone to intercede between me and the Source. I affirmed this realization with the affirmation,

I AM the Master!

Leaving Mount Shasta

When Saint Germain materialized before me in Muir Woods in 1973, he offered liberation; however, when he showed me the suffering of humanity, I chose to remain on Earth to be of service. As a result of that choice he directed me to Mount Shasta, where he said I would receive the training I needed to be of greater assistance to him in his work for humanity.

On this mountain in Northern California I saw the inner temples from which the Masters work for the benefit of humanity. To these temples they sometimes bring their students in etheric form, though on waking the student may have no recollection of the training they receive. The guidance then manifests naturally in their lives at the appropriate time.

I was sent there to learn how to invoke the I AM Presence in daily life, which I learned from Pearl Dorris, former Director of the I AM Sanctuary of San Francisco.[8]

---

[8] Pearl was a personal assistant to Godfrey Ray King, founder of the Saint Germain Foundation and author of *Unveiled Mysteries.* For ad biography of Pearl Dorris read my book: *Lady Master Pearl, My Teacher* (Church of the Seven Rays). The male form is called, in Sanskrit, a *daka.* Read the account of my first meeting and further training with Pearl in *Apprentice to the Masters: Adventures of a Western Mystic, Book II*. In Tibet, Pearl would have been known as a *dakini,* literally a "sky dancer," an enlightened woman who transmits that consciousness to others.

Prior to this, in the late '60s I had learned hatha yoga from Swami Satchitananda and then gone to India, where I received further inspiration from Neem Karoli Baba, Anandamayi Ma, Shivabau Yogi, Sathya Sai Baba, as well as other yogis whose names were unknown. I also studied with various Tibetan Lamas.[9]

After all this spiritual training in Eastern spirituality, I was shocked when at my first meeting with Pearl she said, "Meditate with your eyes open. Bring the light of your I AM Presence down into the center of your being and release it out into the world. This is the beginning of mastery.

"In this inner light you get your guidance. Going to channels for messages only weakens you. Get your own guidance—from the same place the Masters get theirs—in the center of your being. The most direct guidance is non-verbal; you just do the right thing spontaneously. Feel the center of your being, then act in accordance with that feeling."

Perhaps this is what Immanuel Kant meant by the Categorical Imperative (the absolute objective necessity of action)? When all is said and done, the moment arrives and you must act. The time for choice is over and an urge arises. If you are in touch with the center of your being, that urge is your

---

[9] The experiences of my childhood, spiritual awakening, and meetings with Indian gurus and Tibetan Lamas can be read in my autobiographical book: *Search for the Guru: Adventures of a Western Mystic, Book I.*

guidance. I learned to strengthen my connection with that Source through long hours of meditation.

Once I connected with that Presence and learned to call it forth, the Masters put me in situations where I would have to choose between the thoughts going through my mind and the still, silent urging of the heart. I was frequently sent on missions without being given a clear objective—simply told to go. Every action that followed was revealed *in the moment* through the feeling. After more than a three-year probation, Pearl said one day, "It is time for you to begin your service."[10]

For the next forty years I had worked to help those whom Saint Germain sent. On many occasions the Masters sent me on missions to various parts of the world where I was forced to act spontaneously. Through these assignments my lessons and service to the Masters continued.

Now, after all those years in Mount Shasta, I began to feel it was time to leave, but where to go was a mystery. I had been eagerly received in Los Angeles and asked to start a *sangha* (Sanskrit: community) there, but that did not feel right. At moments I thought of returning to India and becoming a yogi like the ones I had lived with in the mountains near Nainital many years before. I

---

[10] Further adventures and training under the Ascended Masters can be read in my autobiographical book: *Apprentice to the Masters: Adventures of a Western Mystic, Book II.*

remembered the Bhrigu *shastri* in Bombay had said I was a teacher in India in a past life and that I would again return to teach there.[11] However, I had come to believe that prediction was symbolic, that the ashram in which I was teaching was an etheric one. I even thought of going back to New York City and sitting on a bench in Central Park to make myself available to anyone passing by who needed to talk.[12]

I felt this immanent departure from Mount Shasta for a year but waited for the inner direction to emerge. Then one day, without effort or planning, the revelation occurred.

---

[11] Bhrigu was one of the seven great sages of pre-Vedic times, and he wrote astrology charts predicting the future lives of over 500,000 souls in a book, the *Bhrigu Samhita*.

[12] An American who used the name Baba Gil had done this. He had left Haight-Ashbury in 1969, gone to India, and eventually taken up residence on a bench on Central Park West. I met him and his followers in Mount Shasta on their visit to see Pearl prior to his journey to New York, and again later on his bench in New York.

Invitation from a Dakini

The revelation to leave my long-time home of Mount Shasta came in the form of a visit by a *dakini*.[13] That is a female spirit capable of transmitting wisdom and enlightenment—in this case a woman by the name of Oceana. She had lived in the *sangha* of a Tibetan Buddhist lama, where she completed the hundred thousand prostrations and other preliminary practices. Eventually, she went to the Insight Meditation Society in Barre, Vermont, where she began a year-long retreat.

Soon after she arrived at the retreat center, the Dalai Lama, who was on a tour of the U.S., came to visit. She never forgot his humor when he looked at their eager faces and said, "Ah, I see you all expect to be enlightened by the end of your retreat!"

"Of course, why not? She thought. They had received the necessary instruction, were dedicated, and had the whole year! However, by the end of the year, she had to admit that attaining enlightenment was harder than it appeared. After the retreat was over, she went to visit a former boyfriend, thinking to rekindle their relationship, but when things didn't work out, she went back to Vermont to begin another

---

[13] *Dakini* (Sanskrit: sky dancer), a female spirit or being who imparts wisdom.

retreat. This time she was going to achieve enlightenment for sure!

To her surprise, she awoke one morning feeling nauseous, and the next day too, and soon realized she was pregnant. What should she do? Should she have an abortion and become a nun for the rest of her life? Or, she could return to the world and see if the Buddhist teachings worked in daily life as a mother?

Determined to prove that she could achieve enlightenment in the midst of family life, she married the father of her child and they moved into a tent. He began constructing a stone house for them, but three years and two more children later, the house was still not completed.

She found that her year in silent meditation had given her a great sense of equanimity that was immensely helpful. However, life had become unworkable. She could no longer raise three children alone in a tent as her husband left much of the week for other work; so, she left him. She then moved into a straw bale house he had built on a nearby hill. There were also several cabins on the property so she opened a Buddhist retreat center.

Eventually, a stupa was built in the center of the property that was blessed by the renowned Tibetan yogi, Dilgo Khyentse Rinpoche. However, she soon discovered that taking care of retreatants in addition to taking care of her three children, was more than she could handle. She stopped scheduling formal retreats but allowed friends to live there or do self-directed retreats.

Now people began to come to visit her, not to learn Buddhist dogma, but because of the wisdom she had acquired and the compassion that radiated from her. She gave counseling to all who came, and often fed them as well. She named the hill on which she lived, Jade Lake, after the mystical lake at the base of Mount Kailash in Tibet, where many great saints had attained liberation.

When she read *Unveiled Mysteries* by Godfre Ray King, she realized the next step in her spiritual path. She saw that Saint Germain was giving the ancient wisdom, through the I AM teachings, in a modern format more suitable to achieving mastery in the Western world. No longer did she need to travel long distances to be with lamas who rarely had time to give private instruction anyway—because she could contact her own I AM Presence and the Ascended Masters anywhere and at any time by looking inward.

She soon began to receive inner guidance to make a pilgrimage to Mount Shasta. It was here where Godfre Ray King had met Saint Germain. Each day the urge to make this pilgrimage became stronger until one day she and a like-minded friend piled in her car and began the drive across the country.

They had now been in the town of Mount Shasta a month, hiking, meditating, and calling to the Masters for guidance. Two days before their planned departure, they went to Soul Connections, the store downtown that sells crystals and pictures of the Masters. On a back shelf she found my autobiographical book, *Apprentice to the Masters: Adventures of a Western Mystic, Book II.*

She felt pulled to buy it, but the cover repelled her, for it showed the author in the pose of Manjusri, Lord of Wisdom, holding aloft the sword of discriminating intelligence. Without seeing the explanation inside about the tantric invocation of oneself as the Deity for the benefit others, she concluded the author must be deluded and left the store without it. As she walked down the sidewalk, she felt Saint Germain place his hand in the center of her chest, and say, "Go back and get that book."

She tried to keep walking, but he insisted, so she went back. That night as she read the book, she realized it contained the revelation for which Saint Germain had sent her to Mount Shasta. The following morning, she phoned.

"May I come to your meditation?"

I didn't realize then, that this phone call was the beginning of the change that would cause my departure.

People used to come every Sunday to meditate at my home. I gave a short talk and after the meditation we would say affirmations to benefit humanity. As Oceana sat on the floor near the right side of my chair, her presence felt familiar, like an old friend. At the end of the gathering she asked, "Have you ever thought of going to New York? I have a spare cabin in the Catskill Mountains, and you are welcome to stay there as long as you want."

In all my years in Mount Shasta I had received only a few groups from New York, yet this summer there had been one group after another—each inviting me to visit, so the idea of New York had been planted in my mind; but none of the offers had felt right until this one.

Next morning, Oceana stopped by on her way out of town, and I realized that I would move to Jade Lake. What I did not realize was that to sort out my possessions would take almost a year.

When the moment arrived to depart this home, where I had been trained and nurtured by the Masters, I hesitated. As I drove toward the freeway I wondered, *can the Masters really want me to leave my home?*

I happened to glance at the dashboard as if seeking guidance there, and the clock flashed 11:33, a number that had always been special, and I knew that was my confirmation. I entered the freeway and began the long, arduous drive eastward. As I drove, I affirmed,

I am the Presence of the Living God driving this car.

I am the Ascended Council of Light in action!
Come forth in and through all the communities and states through which I pass and bless all the inhabitants!

I am going where I am meant to go,
doing what I am meant to do,
for I am God in action here!

The Light of God never fails!
The Light of God never fails!
The Light of God never fails!
And I am that Light!

I spent the first night near Nevada City, where I was welcomed by a group of Yogananda devotees, then drove on to Colorado Springs, where I stayed with Scott Sanford and his wife, Trish, in their home on the side of Cheyenne Mountain. Scott asked me to give a talk to his students he was teachings about the Masters; and I then continued driving east, stopping here and there to talk to other groups.

Finally, I reached the East Coast, and as I drove up the steep dirt road to Jade Lake, I felt the welcoming energy of the Masters. From this wide-open mountain top, it seemed there was no place to go but up and I wondered, *is this where I will complete my ascension?*

However, after Oceana settled me in the cozy straw bale cabin with a view of the mountains, I felt more relaxed. She soon asked me to lead an I AM study group in her sanctuary, and I began to feel I had a new home. Every Sunday morning people arrived, and I gave a short talk followed by a meditation on bringing the I AM Presence into the human world. We ended by reading from *Unveiled Mysteries* or the *"I AM" Discourses,* both brought forth by Godfre Ray King.

Every morning I rose before the sun and sat in meditation. As the rosy-fingered dawn spread against the backdrop of the mountains, I went outside and sat on the stone wall in front of the cabin to greet the rising sun. Qi Gong practice followed, which grounded the energy. Then I wandered down through the field, past the stupa depicting the mind of the Buddha, to Oceana's house. We sipped coffee and discussed the nature of reality, inevitably ending with the realization that all phenomena are empty and devoid of inherent meaning.

I would then go back to my desk overlooking the valley and work on my next book. In the afternoon, I went next door to the woodshed and split logs for the evening fire that would keep the cabin warm until sunrise.

Under the encouragement of Saint Germain, I began writing about my experiences in Tibet. He encouraged this book as a vehicle for the ancient teachings that he wanted presented in the West. Usually these teachings were given in Tibetan or only to those who had years of training with a lama and had completed all the prostrations and other extensive preliminary practices.

Oceana was excited about the project, and her enthusiasm kept the creative fire flowing. I began reliving the experiences I had in Tibet and the book flowed effortlessly. It finally emerged as *My Search in Tibet for the Secret Wish-Fulfilling Jewel*—the jewel being the inner Christ Light, or in Sanskrit, the *Cintamani* Stone (*jyoti*).[14]

---

[14] The Wish-Fulfilling Jewel is known in Theosophy as the Philosopher's Stone. Tibetan legend tells of a meteor that fell to earth thousands of years ago, and that possession of a fragment gives the owner magical qualities; however, no one in Tibet claims to have such a fragment. Today new age entrepreneurs sell cheap tektites, claiming they are cintamani stones imbued with magical qualities.

Come Along

A huge poplar tree swaying above the roof was the only thing bothering me. I had a vision of it blowing down on the cabin some night while I slept. Many smaller poplar trees had already fallen along the stone wall that ran behind the cabin. Here in the Catskills, these trees seemed to grow on every hillside. The one behind the cabin, though, was the largest on the mountain. As I watched it sway, I wondered *how much longer do I have?*

I sat on my futon at night meditating, aware of this tree swaying only twenty feet away, knowing that at any moment it could crash through the roof.

I confessed my fear to Oceana and she called a tree removal company. They said it was beyond their ability. It would take a hydraulic bucket to lift a man up to cut the branches first before the tree could be felled. That would be expensive, and all the other people Oceana phoned were booked for months. I had no choice but to call to my Higher Self and affirm:

I am the Presence of God removing this tree in perfect Divine order!

And I prayed to the Ascended Masters:

Beloved Masters, please bring about the perfect Divine plan for the removal of this tree. If there is no danger, then remove my fear. If the tree is going to fall and it is my time to leave this body, please take me peacefully.

Then it came to mind, *perhaps the purpose of this situation is simply to help me overcome fear? I know I am where God wants me, so whatever happens must be the will of God.*

One day I saw Hans, a friend of Oceana's crossing the field. I had meet him briefly at Oceana's. When he saw me, he asked how I was doing.

"I'd be doing better if that tree were not leaning over my cabin."

"Wow, that's a big one…those poplars blow down so easily," he said, squinting up at the tree, then continued off across the field.

A week later, two men appeared in the field, looking toward the cabin, but soon left. A few days later I was sitting at my desk, I saw Hans and these same two men approaching. Each carried a device resembling a block and tackle rigged to a metal cable. Hans gripped a large chainsaw.

"What's up, Hans?"

"I've come to take down your tree," he said.

"But that will take a hydraulic bucket," I said, repeating what the tree service had said.

"Nah, I can do it with these come-alongs," he said, nodding at the devices his companions carried. "I just finished a course in how to do this at the community college."

Oh, great, he's using my cabin as an experiment, I thought.

"Does Oceana know about this?" I asked.

"Sure, she'll be here in a minute."

They went behind the cabin and hitched the two come-alongs high up on the poplar and secured the ends to two other trees. Before I could go back inside and remove my computer in case things didn't go as planned, Hans throttled the chainsaw and began cutting the trunk.

"Pull on your ropes!" he shouted to the other men. As they pulled, the trunk began to straighten.

"I'm going to set it down right over there," Hans said, pointing over the stone wall where there was a clearing; but his optimism was cut short as the nearest come-along bent and its main gear popped out, letting the tree sag back to its original position.

"It's not going to work!" one of the men shouted.

But Hans remained positive, not to be deterred. He went to a neighbor's barn, where he knew another come-along hung on the wall. In this rural community where people's lives depended on each other, there was an unspoken agreement among friends that you could take what you needed as long as you put it back.

In twenty minutes, he returned with the replacement. He hooked it up, gave the order to pull, and the tree straightened once again. He fired up the chain saw and continued cutting the trunk, first on the side where he wanted the tree to fall, then on the opposite side. He then pounded a steel wedge into one of the cuts, stepped back, and commanded, "Pull hard!"

The tree swayed, and with an amazing CRACK flipped over backward and crashed over the stone wall exactly where Hans had said he would drop it.

Oceana, who had been watching, looked at me in amazement. She must have wondered like me if the cabin was going to be demolished. She shouted ecstatically to Hans, "Congratulations, you did it!"

"Of course I did it, why not?

The Hour of the Spider

After I was spared a tree falling on the roof of my cabin, things went well at Jade Lake—for a while—until I was faced with another life-threatening experience. Ironically it was the consequence of Oceana's adherence to the Buddhist belief in non-harmfulness know as *ahimsa*.[15] Oceana adhered to this belief so absolutely that she picked the fleas off her cats by hand, took them outside, and prayed for their liberation as she set them free.

She had asked me to adhere to it also, and I agreed. *But, what should I do about the spiders in the corners of the woodshed door?* I had to duck to miss them each time I went to get firewood.

One day, a load of firewood was delivered in front of the cabin and I began stacking the logs in the shed. I made it a tantric practice that I dedicated for the benefit of others, praying all people would be warm during the coming winter. With each load I recited a mantra, making the repetitive stacking of logs a meditation practice similar to the observation of the breath in vipassana.

---

[15]*Ahimsa,* non-harmfulness, is a primary doctrine of Buddhism and Hinduism. However, in the Hindu classic, the *Mahabharata,* warfare is approved under dharmic circumstances, and members of the warrior cast are allowed to consume meat. *Vairagya,* a related concept meaning absence of desire, can also mean letting go of attachment to arbitrary concepts of right and wrong.

I became so immersed in this novel application of tantra that I forgot to duck crossing the threshold into the shed. I felt a spider drop inside my shirt. It tickled, then, after an hour, it began to itch. I asked the spider for forgiveness and prayed it would find a new home, though I suspected it might have been crushed when I took off my shirt. Since it was too late to restore the web, I ignored the itch and went back to chanting and stacking wood.

A week later, the itch still persisted and grew worse. I took herbs and homeopathic remedies, but it gradually morphed into a dull pain. I kept thinking the pain would go away, but instead it grew stronger. The pain became so intense that when I lay down at night, I could only sleep an hour or two. I wondered again, as I had when I arrived at Jade Lake, *is it time to leave this body and move on to a higher world?*

I prayed for guidance, yet received none, so I began researching painless methods of suicide. I tried to hide the pain from Oceana, yet perhaps she knew. One morning a stranger showed up at the door of the cabin bearing a jar of Ayahuasca. As he handed it to me, he said, "I heard you might need this." Then he turned and left.

I had heard about the healing potential of this murky brown mixture of plants from the Amazon, and since I felt I was going to die soon anyway, I thought *why not try it? What can I lose?*

I remembered a friend who had gone to the Amazon and stayed with the Shipibo Indians. He took the sacrament with them as part of a ceremony and when he came back, he looked twenty years younger. I asked him the secret of his youthful appearance and he said, "I saw that every emotional wound of my past was still stored in the muscles, tendons, and bones of my body. The Ayahuasca brought all those repressed wounds to the surface to be looked at and dissolved. The pain I was holding onto was making me old. I had to forgive everyone for everything, and also ask forgiveness for all I had done. Once that old stuff was gone, I felt reborn."

Thinking how it had benefitted him, I prayed to Saint Germain for guidance. *Perhaps he was even the one who had sent the Ayahuasca?* I continued to feel I should take it, so I went on the recommended diet for three days, eating only cooked vegetables and rice, even omitting salt (that many shamans say closes down the chakras).

On the appointed day, I set up an altar in the back room of the cabin and leaned against a wall, facing pictures of Jesus, Mother Mary, and the Maha Chohan. Slowly, I sipped the brown liquid, which did not taste as bad as I had been told. In fact, I even liked it. In twenty minutes, I had consumed three fourths of the jar's contents and felt instinctively to stop.

Suddenly, an Amazonian shaman wearing three feathers in his hair, appeared to my left. He shook a rattle in my direction and disappeared, and then the ground began to shake.

An earthquake? In New York? Looking at the glass of water on the shrine, I saw the surface was motionless, so I realized it was not the earth that was moving, but my mind.

I closed my eyes and found myself sitting astride a huge black Anaconda. I wrapped my arms around it as it undulated through the jungle. A jaguar jumped in front of us, then disappeared in the undergrowth. Birds with brilliant plumage swooped down from the jungle canopy and shot past us. Overwhelmed, I lay down on the floor.

A brilliant light-show reminiscent of a 60s rock concert began, with brilliant colors flashing through my mind. I felt abandoned and alone in this strange world, and called out, "Mother Mary, help me!"

Suddenly she was there, her loving arms around my shoulders, enveloping me in her motherly embrace. The fear and emptiness left, and I was filled with light. Everything was going to be alright.

I was in a cavern with many massive oak doors that I wanted to throw open and see what lay inside. I pulled one open and saw heaps of gold coins ready to be taken, but knew this was not why I was here. In another room an orgy was going on—and a naked woman beckoned me to enter. Again, I slammed the door. In another room people were waiting to heap me with praise and honor, but again I closed the door. Stepping back from the row of doors, I called out,

"Hear me, O Spirit of Ayahuasca! I am not here to pursue this illusory world of samsara. I did not take Ayahuasca for this!"

A woman's voice whispered in my ear, "Why did you take it then?"

"For healing…I want healing!"

A doctor stood before me. He wore traditional green hospital scrubs, green cap, and a white surgical mask over his face. He stepped forward as if to operate, but instead of a scalpel he pointed his index finger at my side—at the place where the pain was most intense—and a beam of rainbow light shot into my side. "Take Una de Gato and Chancre Piedra," he said, then disappeared.[16]

The pain was gone, so I sat up and drank the glass of water on the alter. Still feeling lightheaded, I walked downhill through the field and past the stupa. I was eager to tell Oceana about the amazing healing I had received.

Weeks later, when I told a Vedic astrologer about this experience, he said, "The spider is a symbol of the *Ketu dasha* (cycle) you are going through, so, rather than evil, try to see the spider as an ally sent to teach you, to awaken you to some hidden part of yourself."

---

[16] Amazonian herbs used to strengthen the immune system.

Eckhart Tolle at Walmart

Being on retreat I avoided socializing. However, I still had to go into town every couple of weeks for supplies. As winter set in, I realized I needed a windshield scraper. The most likely place to find this was at Walmart, but I postponed going into Oneonta, where the nearest stores were, as long as possible. Finally, I descended my idyllic hilltop for the mystifying corridors of Walmart, the store that offered all the material things that promised to fulfil the American dream—what Henry Miller called *The Air-Conditioned Nightmare.*

On my way through the parking lot, I took deep breaths of fresh air in preparation for the synthetic environment ahead. I prayed to Saint Germain for guidance and affirmed,

> *I am going where I am meant to go,
> doing what I am meant to do.*

Inside was the world of *the ten thousand things*, probably now ten million things, most of which I would never need.[17] To my dismay, there were no signs indicating where plastic scrapers might be, not even a sign for Auto Parts. Wandering around, I became more and more lost, and felt close to panic

---

[17] Taoist, as well as ancient Greek philosophy, uses the number ten-thousand as symbolic of the world of maya—the endless quest for material things, none of which bring lasting happiness.

when I could no longer see an exit. A huge woman in tights in a motorized cart nearly ran into me, and I backed up into a man who looked as though he had crawled out of the bushes behind the store. I said a quick affirmation,

> *I am the presence of the Ascended Masters and Ascended Master Friends raised up before me, bringing about the Divine Plan here right now.*[18]

I looked in vain for someone to ask directions from. Despairing of finding the scraper, I turned to look for an exit. Then there was a short man wearing the blue jacket of a Walmart employee in front of me stocking shelves. I approached and said, "Excuse me, I need help."

He turned and I found myself face to face with Eckhart Tolle, the author of *The Power of Now.*[19] I had seen him interviewed on The Oprah Winfrey Show and his gnome-like face was unmistakable. Speechless, I looked for a name tag to confirm his identity, but he had none.

---

[18] Ascended Master Friends are those individuals the Masters can use to help fulfill some higher plan, often without that person's awareness. These people often appear at the right place and time to provide assistance to other students of the Masters.
[19] Eckhart Tolle, a Canadian resident born in Germany in 1948, was according to a New York Times article in 2008, "the most popular spiritual author in the United States."

I thought, *he must be doing research for his next book—how to achieve mastery in mundane life, even as a Walmart employee!*

This man whose face was in every bookstore window stared at me and asked in a German accent, "Yes...can I do something for you?"

Shocked, I stammered, "That's OK...thanks anyway," and continued walking down the aisle. Eventually, I came to a sign that said Auto Parts, and there was an ice scraper. I grabbed it and walked back the way I had come, intending now to talk with the famous writer, and introduce myself. I wanted to ask, *what have you learned working at Walmart?* For someone so sensitive, working there would certainly be a challenge and require great patience—forcing him to put into practice his teachings on how to live in the present moment.

However, when I got back to where he had been working, he was gone. I searched the neighboring aisles, but he had disappeared. I finally found the front of the store again, paid for the scraper, and left. When I reached my truck, I sat for a while, pondering my unexpected encounter with the New York Times best-selling author.

Next day I went back, determined to find Eckhart and talk with him, but he was not there. I wondered, *maybe he only needed to work that one day to learn what he needed.* I vowed to watch for his next book and see if it would be titled something like *In the Now at Walmart.*

Since I was in town anyway, I decided to go to the Latte Lounge, a local student hangout, which shared an interior door with the neighboring bookstore. While waiting for my order, I looked at the best-sellers. On the top shelf was Eckhart Tolle's book, *The Power of Now*. As I looked into the author's face, I heard Saint Germain laugh, and I realized then that he was the one I had met at Walmart.

That experience changed forever the way I experienced, not only Walmart, but many other potentially stressful situations. Just knowing that I am never out of the Master's mind, even at Walmart, was a big help.

A Visit from Two Masters

I had been on retreat in the Catskill Mountains of New York for almost the last three years, during which time I finished three books: *My Search in Tibet for the Secret Wish-Fulfilling Jewel,* an account of my travels in Tibet written at the request of Saint Germain, to bring forth certain ancient teachings of the Far East. I also edited the teachings of Jesus, under his supervision, in *I AM the Living Christ,* which gave his words in an up to date language that referred to God the Mother as well as Father. Lastly, I edited *Step by Step*, a collection of powerful I AM Discourses that had been given to my teacher, Pearl, and which she had passed on to me. I had weathered three cold winters with snow piled high against the windows, and now it seemed everything had come to a standstill. I wondered again, as when I first arrived on the mountain, *perhaps my work is finished and I can complete my ascension?*

That night as I sat on my futon meditating, two Ascended Masters appeared out of nowhere, El Morya and his companion, Kuthumi. Not wasting time on pleasantries, Kuthumi said, "So, you really want to leave your body? We have come for your decision."

Finally, here is my chance, I thought, but instead of saying what my human self wanted, liberation, the voice of my soul said, "I want whatever will be of most benefit to humanity."

"Very well then, we will tell the boss," El Morya concluded with a wry sense of humor, knowing I would understand the boss to be the Lord Maha Chohan—the one overseeing the Chohans of the Seven Rays, and my immediate supervisor. The two Masters nodded and disappeared as abruptly as they had arrived.[20]

Weeks passed without further clarification or any answer to my question. I thought I could help humanity more by ascending, but the "boss" might have thought I could accomplish more by remaining in embodiment. I waited every night for the Masters to return with clarification, but in vain.

Finally, since I was not told anything one way or the other, late one night I decided to ascend on my own volition. I decided *I will attain the Rainbow Body like the yogis of Tibet!*

I threw my attention inward with all my focus and raised the inner light of my chakras upward as an offering to my Christ Self, then raised all the centers further toward the I AM Presence, bringing all the lights together. I knew that when all the centers merged the ascension would be complete.

I affirmed,

I am now dissolving the human self into the Higher Self!

---

[20] The Masters are not the solemn, long-faced individuals often portrayed by Theosophists, but are embodiments of love who often manifest mirth and have a definite sense of humor.

A flash of dazzling light suddenly filled the room, and the entire hilltop lit up as though illuminated by the sun at noon. A hiss of electricity surged through the room and I passed out.

In the morning I woke to find to my disappointment that I still had a physical body. When the lights did not turn on, I realized the cabin must have been hit by lightning as the wires in the walls had melted.

It was clear then, *I am still meant to be here. It is time to return to Mount Shasta, where the Masters have further work for me to accomplish.*

The Maha Chohan had delivered his answer on a thunderbolt like the Greek Gods of ancient mythology, and I hoped the Masters had enjoyed a good laugh.

Zen Mechanic

On a cold fall morning I prepared for the long drive back across the country. My seventeen-year-old truck had been making strange sounds, so I took it in to be checked out. I didn't want to be stranded by the roadside in the middle of Kansas. Although I knew the Masters would be with me, I knew it was still up to me to me to take care of the material plane as much as I could.

I pulled up in front of Jim's Garage and Jim greeted me with a smile, "What seems to be the problem?"

"The front end is making strange sounds."

"Well, we replaced the wheel bearings already."

I was shocked that he remembered what repairs he had made six months ago, and wondered why someone with so sharp a mind wanted to work in a cold, greasy garage; then again, I realized he worked with his father with whom he had a good relationship, and lived on a beautiful hillside with his wife and two children just a few minute walk up the hill. He had a good life.

Jim put the truck on the lift, yanked the right wheel back and forth, scratched his head, and said, "Say, you didn't buy those cheap bearings last time, did you?"

I had come in before when the truck was making a noise, and he had sent me into town to the parts store and the salesman had shown me two sets of bearings, one expensive, one cheap. I remembered wondering about the difference since they both looked the same.

"I bought the cheap ones...is that bad?" I confessed.

A quizzical smile appeared on his face—the knowing look of a Zen master, and he said,

It is what it is.

His reply reverberated throughout my being. I felt absolved—not only of making the wrong decision, but of all the mistakes I had made, all the times my mother had said I had done the wrong thing. Now it seemed that there were no wrong decisions, only lessons. I felt accepted as a person, mistakes and all. This mechanic had absolved me of my sins on a par with any priest.

Poking around under the front end of my truck, Jim suddenly shouted, "Hey, guess what? It's not the bearings...it's the pinions. You have to go back into town to the parts store and get new ones."

Relieved, I went to the parts store one more time, and with great satisfaction bought the expensive parts. After the pinions were installed, Jim said, as though delivering a blessing personally from the Masters, "Now you won't be stranded in the middle of Kansas!"

I gave Oceana a hug, knowing I would miss her. She had been a dakini who was a constant inspiration, and had given me this beautiful retreat space for the past three years. My heart beat wildly as I climbed into the truck. Finally I turned on the ignition and drove off across the rutted field without looking back. Soon I was on the freeway headed west.

My Spacecraft

Dreading the long drive back to California, I wished I had the small space craft I had been given in a vivid out-of-the body experience years ago. I knew in the future that means of travel would become a reality. I wondered, *why don't they return that spacecraft to me now?*

The first night of the drive, I stopped in New Jersey to visit a friend who does radio interviews. He wanted to interview me about my experiences with the Masters.

As I pulled into his driveway at the end of rural lane, he came out and greeted me excitedly, "Peter, last night you visited me in a UFO! I thought it was only a dream, but this morning when I went out to the garden, I found a round impression in the plants the same size as your craft!"

"Sorry about crushing the plants," I said.

"Well, at least it confirms it was not a dream. If you had parked the craft in the driveway it wouldn't have left an imprint."

Even though I joked about not landing on the plants in future visits, I felt this was a confirmation I was operating on more levels than I was allowed to remember. I knew the time was not far off when I would be using this type of craft in full earthly awareness.

Love Opens the Door

I continued west on Interstate-70 and a couple of days later I passed through Columbia, Missouri. I decided to gas up at a small, solitary station about ten miles east of the city. As I got out of the truck, I noticed the time on the dashboard clock was wrong as I had crossed into a new time zone. Digging around in the glove box, I found a ball point pen I could use to push the time reset button. However, I had to reinsert the ignition key to activate the electrical system.

After I set the clock back an hour, I went inside to pay for a tank of gas. As I waited in line, I couldn't help but notice that the young woman behind the counter was scowling at everyone. She was in such a bad mood I dreaded having to talk to her. However, I realized that if I had her job, I'd be in a bad mood too, and visualized her surrounded in a pink cloud of divine love.

When I finally arrived in front of her she snapped, "Do you want something else?" I wanted to tell her "lighten up," but instead said, "No, just the gas," as I felt she could explode at the slightest provocation.

I returned to the truck and reached into my pocket for the keys, but they were gone. Peering through the truck window, I saw them hanging from the ignition, where I had left them when I changed the time.

I was locked out. My worst fear of being stranded in a desolate place was now realized. I called immediately to Saint Germain and the other Masters,

*Saint Germain and great host of
Ascended Masters, please come forth now and help me!*

I am the open door that no man can shut!

I am, I am, I know that I am, come forth now!

Since no Master appeared with a universal master key, I felt I had no choice but to go back inside and ask for help. I dreaded facing the angry woman behind the counter, but realized I had no choice. There was no other living being around to ask for help.

When I approached, she scowled and asked, "So whadya want now?"

"I locked my keys in my truck," I stammered, cringing as I waited for her wrathful reply, but the moment she sensed my desperation, she became transformed. She was no longer a wrathful dragon spewing fire but transformed before my eyes into a compassionate Goddess.

"Oh, you poor thing…I will help you," she said, enveloping me in a feeling of maternal goodness.

In a second, she pulled out her cell phone and found two locksmiths near Columbia and gave me their phone numbers; but when I called, both said they were busy. She then asked a man mopping the floor in back who I hadn't seen before, and he gave me another number. The man who answered said he would be there in twenty minutes. True to his word, a truck pulled up and a burly man jumped out. Without a word of greeting, he jammed a wedge in the door and whacked it with a sledge hammer, popping the door open.

"That'll be forty bucks, our minimum charge," he said, apologetically. I paid and he handed me the receipt. After he drove off, I looked at the receipt and was stunned to see the name, Master Locksmiths.

Before leaving, I wanted to thank the woman who had helped me. She was now a different person than the one I had first encountered. She effused love and goodness as she asked, "Did you get it fixed, honey?"

"Yes, thanks to you,"

I wanted to show my thanks in some material way but didn't want to hurt her feelings by offering her money. Nonetheless, I finally reached into my pocket and handed her a folded-up five-dollar bill.

"Oh, no, I couldn't accept anything," she said holding her hands up.

"I know you helped me out of the goodness of your heart, but we all have to make a living and it would make me feel good if you would take this as a small token of my gratitude," I said.

She finally took the gift and with a compassionate smile said, "Now, y'all take care of yourself, ya'hear!"

With love in my heart, I said goodbye to this dakini. I wanted to ask for her name and address so I could send her a postcard when I got back to California, but shyness prevented me.

I went back to the truck and started the engine. As I pulled out of the parking lot, I noticed the name of the place on a sign: "Love's Travel Stop."

The Man in the Hoodie

Winter was coming and I was going to be homeless. I had returned to Mount Shasta to sub-let a promised house, but after a month of readying it for Ascended Master retreats, my landlord was evicted, and I had to leave as well. A friend finally heard of my plight and temporarily offered a spare room. This was not the welcome home I had expected from the Masters. I had returned to serve them as I had in the past; but now it felt like they had shut the door. A feeling of rejection plunged me into a dark night of the soul and I asked myself *what have I done wrong?*

When I called on the Masters in the past, everything fell into place. I was sure I had followed their guidance, yet instead of having a home where I could meditate, write, and teach as in the past, I was in a noisy condominium complex with people coming and going at all hours.

Adding to my gloom were the new clothes I had ordered. My old ones had holes from carrying firewood every day. The pants were baggy and the shirt was not the color shown in the picture. I wanted to return them but didn't want to spend the time. Pondering what to do, I decided to get a cup of coffee. As I walked up Old McCloud Road toward Seven Suns Café, I thought with every step, "I hate this outfit…I hope nobody I know sees me."

As I walked, I had a conversation in my mind with Saint Germain, telling him that I didn't understand why the Masters had brought me back to

Mount Shasta; not only did I not have a satisfactory place to live and work, but I didn't like my appearance either.

As I reached Mount Shasta Boulevard, with the café across the street, a young man wearing a black hoodie looked at me. I turned my back. These hoodies had become popular among many young people after the shooting of a young African-American who had been wearing one. Not only did they hide a person's face so it would be hard to identify someone who had committed a crime, but they seemed to beg for conflict, the black color also blended with darkness. So, I gave the young man a wide clearance. Yet, he continued staring at me. As I waited for the traffic to clear so I could cross the street, he said, "Hey, dude, I like your outfit!"

"What?" I said, incredulous, as I had been revolving over and over in my mind as I walked, *I hate this outfit.*

He repeated, "I like your outfit. In fact, I like your whole aura! You have the energy of a famous writer, someone like Hemingway."

I was speechless, not only that he liked my appearance, but that he named the writer whose literary style I most admired. I finally turned to face the hooded person heaping me with compliments. I wanted to say something kind in return, but there was no one there—I was alone on the street corner.

That's strange! But, what would I have said, anyway? I would not have lied to say I liked his outfit too, which consisted of athletic shorts, flip-flops, and the hoodie.

I erased the incident from my mind and crossed the street to the café. With coffee in hand, I went outside to see if the strange fellow had reappeared, but he was nowhere to be seen. As I pondered the strange encounter, I realized I felt better—at least one person thought I was OK and even had good energy.

I awakened next morning feeling the presence of Saint Germain. "So, you didn't like my outfit?" he laughed, and was gone. I was ecstatic.

Circumstances changed after that. I was offered a house in the woods, perfect for a writer. I moved in, feeling I was once again in a place where I could work. But *what is my work?*

International Visitors

The Masters answered my question about the nature of my work with events rather than with an audible message. Within a week of moving into my new house, people began showing up from all over the world, coming in groups of from three to fifteen. In two weeks over fifty people arrived from China, Russia, the Netherlands, Ireland, Brazil, and a few from the U.S. Most were women.

I asked what brought them, and they said my books, YouTube videos, or my website.[21] Others said they were guided to Mount Shasta in dreams or visions. Most were seeking guidance from the Masters, but some simply wanted to make a heart connection with me.

When someone who is sincere and has an open heart sits in front of me, often my Higher Self or a Master pours a blessing from my heart center to theirs—the same direct transmission that used to happen when I sat with Pearl. The awareness of this inner flame is what provides guidance and is the foundation of Mastery.

In the heart center you realize your oneness with others, what the Buddhists call *bodhicitta*. It is what my teacher called the Pearl of Great Price, and what Trungpa Rinpoche called the "soft spot."

---

[21] www.I-AM-Teachings.com has books and video teachings available for download, also a contact form to reach the author.

It is that center beneath the sternum, where people feel, not only joy, but also get in touch with their emotional wounds. There, in that tender spot, is where the needed healing occurs. We come back lifetime after lifetime to heal those wounds and transform ignorance into wisdom. Mothers feel that soft spot spontaneously as their love flows forth to their children. We all have that ability, but it takes focus upon that Light in the center of that soft spot.

Maharajji Appears

A woman showed up at my cabin who was very learned in Theosophical studies and I wondered, *what could I possibly teach this woman?*

However, the more she talked I began to see how confused she was. Theosophy and many occult studies keep people in the mind without teaching how to observe the mind.[22] Despite her knowledge of metaphysics, she was obsessed with self-doubt and unable to hold one thought for more than a few seconds.

After a while I had enough and asked her to let go of her thoughts and focus on her breathing. Gradually her mind slowed, and she began to feel her center. It was then the Masters began to pour their light through her, and she became translucent. Love then began to emanate from her heart.

She sat up in surprise, "Who is that fat Indian guy in the blanket?"

"What guy?"

---

[22] None of the well-known Theosophists I am aware of practiced meditation as known in the Far East; likewise, none of the channels of the Masters from Godfrey Ray King on down through Elizabeth Clare Prophet or her later imitators practiced meditation. Hence, it is doubtful any of them attained enlightenment, so never personally attained direct perception of truth. It is easier to "channel" supposedly enlightened beings than to know the truth oneself.

"Why the guy sitting in your chair! You disappeared, and there was a fat, bald, guy there."

By her description, I knew she saw Neem Karoli Baba, whose old blanket I had draped over the back of the chair. When I showed her a photo of him, she said, "That's him!"

This was the guru known as Maharajji, who had transformed Harvard professor, Richard Alpert, into the new age spiritual teacher, Baba Ram Dass.[23] Since he seemed to have not paid much attention to me when I sat at his feet almost fifty years ago, for him to appear now was a surprise. I had not had contact with him since he served me chai during a private audience with him at his ashram in Vrindavan, India in 1971.[24] In fact, during the six months I had hung out with him, he had seemed determined to ignore me. He did everything possible to discourage my seeing him as my guru—which made me feel doubly rejected, as everyone around him worshipped him as a God. At the end, he was so determined to turn my attention inward and find the guru within that he had picked up a rock and threatened to throw it at me. *What is he doing here now in my chair?*

---

[23] Author of *Be Here Now* (Lama Foundation, 1971). Neem Karoli Baba, called Maharajji by his followers (1900-1973).

[24] Read my account of this private meeting with Neem Karoli Baba in *Search for the Guru: Adventures of a Western Mystic, Book I.* He died a year later on September 11, 1973.

That night I sat at my desk writing, when suddenly I felt Maharajji's unique presence. His energy grew until I found myself turning into him. Soon I had a protruding belly encircled in a white *dhoti*—and his love filled my being.

"What do you want? Why are you coming to me now after all these years? Is there something you want to tell me?" I asked.

As I listened intently, I heard "We are one."

This is what he wanted me to realize back in 1971. This was the answer to the question he had asked one day when I entered his room. He had asked, "Who are you?"

A few weeks later, on the night of my birthday, I woke to find him sitting on the edge of the bed. He looked into my eyes and answered the question I had been asking the Masters: When can I leave my body?"

"I want you to stay in your body…you have work to do here," he said.

He drew my head against his chest in a hug, then I was alone. I sat up and meditated on what had happened. I knew now what he wanted me to realize a half century ago.

This highly revered Indian saint was now obviously a member of the Ascended Council of Light, and working with Saint Germain.[25] In the

---

[25] I have used here the term Ascended Council of Light to replace the traditional Great White Brotherhood, as these beings

ascended state cultural differences disappear—for in Heaven there are no religions. The appearance of this Master in the form that had been known as Maharajji was merely an illusion used to convey a message.

Maharajji (Neem Karoli Baba)

---

are of all genders and races. The color white refers only to the robes in which they appear and the light they emanate.

The Place of Great Awakening

I felt so blessed by the sacred teachings the Masters had given me over the years that I wanted to make them more available. One day I realized the best place to start was in helping people observe their own minds. Various forms of self-observation underlie all spiritual practice.

I had learned a powerful method from Trungpa Rinpoche that combines *shinay* (stillness) with *vipassana* (self-inquiry). It begins with the observation of the breath and with the eyes slightly open.

When I ran into Rich Anderson, the owner of the Herb and Health store, and told him of my desire to teach *vipassana,* he offered the basement of his building as a meditation hall. He said the Dalai Lama had appeared in a dream and said he had a project for him—but didn't tell him what the project was. He thought now this was what the Dali Lama intended?

Since names have a great influence on the energy invoked, I named the center The Place of Great Awakening. If you go someplace to meditate, would you rather think, "I am going to the basement of the herb store," or "I am going to the Place of Great Awakening." Of course the great awakening is to the realization of your True Self—that you are a Buddha.

We met every Thursday night and I gave a brief introduction for all the newcomers:

1) Sit motionless, back straight, eyes slightly open and looking comfortably downward.[26]

2) Hands can rest palm downward on the knees or one palm in the other, resting in the lap.

3) Feel the in-breath and out-breath, the rise and fall of your chest.

4) Don't think about anything except the feeling of the breath. If a thought arises, label it "thinking," and return to the feeling of the breath. Do not try to control the breath; just allow it to find its natural rhythm.

5) Let your awareness sink to the center of your chest.

6) Allow your mind to expand outward without limit.

Gradually, the mind and breath slow—with longer and longer gaps between thoughts. In those

---

[26] The southern Buddhist, forest tradition, teaches a slightly different form, with eyes closed, where one observes the sensations in various parts of the body. Although this teaches concentration and stillness of mind, I have not seen this method as effective for cutting through the illusion of the emotions as the eyes-open method.

gaps will be moments of pure awareness, free of all concepts. During this process the following dialogue may occur between different aspects of your mind:

What is going on?
I'm meditating.
Who is meditating?
Me!
Who is that?

As you continue this process of inquiry you will discover that the self you are examining is an illusion. The being you truly are is beyond name, form, and thought. You are birthless, deathless, primordially pure, and free.

Whenever the mind wanders, keep returning to the breath. Observation of the breath is not an end in itself, only a means—a doorway to the infinite.

This is the basic method that Siddhartha Gautama used to become a Buddha, an awakened one. As you practice self-observation you too will become a Buddha.

I thought it would be easy to teach this method and that everyone would practice according to the simple instructions. I was shocked when I discovered people were doing a variety of other practices. Some were praying to Jesus or visualizing world peace—both good practices, but which generally do not lead to self-realization.

There were also those who wanted to change the form of seating, having everyone face the wall as in some Zen practices, while others demanded to sit in a circle to be more equal. Some wanted an elaborate alter with statues and tapestries of Tibetan Deities, while others wanted simply a vase containing a single flower; a bouquet would have been too much distraction.

I tried to take everyone's requests into consideration, but after a while I realized that, as Trungpa Rinpoche had said, spiritual practice is not democratic. You cannot teach yourself what you do not know. There has to be a structured focus to keep the ego from taking over. When lighting a candle, you place it in a glass lantern—a form that protects the flame from being extinguished by passing breezes.

This basic meditation is the foundation on which later practices can be added. Although there can be some benefit from simply reciting an affirmation (prayers expressed in the "I Am…." format), without the awareness of the True Self, the constant repetition of affirmations to get what you desire simply magnifies the ego. This is the danger of the contemporary practice using the "Law of Attraction." However, the best use of affirmation is to help you manifest in your life what God already wants to give you. The plant does not struggle to produce the flower—it blossoms out of its own basic nature.

I was also shocked to discover that many of the people who came to meditate were trying to escape some pain. They sought, not so much enlightenment, as an end to their suffering.

I began to suggest that when people sit down on the cushion, they take a few deep breaths and ask, "What am I feeling?"

Reduce that statement to its simplest expression, no more than three words, preferably one, such as loneliness. It might also be fear, anger, frustration, or a health problem. Identify the problem first, then you can work with, and clear it.

As your mind becomes still, you realize you are not the only one with this pain or problem. Millions of others on earth at this very moment are feeling exactly what you are. By transmuting it within yourself, you transmute it for them also. This is the practice of giving and taking, what the Tibetans call *tonglen*. In this way you transmute suffering into joy, aversion into equanimity, and ego-cherishing into compassion for others.

To do this, still the mind. As you exhale, send rays of golden light from the sun in your chest to the hearts of those, like yourself, with your same pain. See your light filling their hearts, minds, and bodies—alleviating their suffering. As you inhale, again realize your oneness with them, but end with the light in the center of your chest.

A Cat Returns a Favor

Years ago, I had to move out of my place and a friend let me stay at her house in town until I could find a new home. I was walking down the street to the post office when I heard a cat crying. I thought it belonged to a neighbor, so I ignored it. Next day I heard the pitiful cry again. I looked all over the neighborhood yet was unable to find the source of the pitiful crying. The following day a cold drizzle began to fall and the cry took on a sense of desperation.

Unable to ignore this cry for help any longer, I followed the cries to a neighbor's high fence. Peering over, I saw two Doberman Pincers looking up into a tall Oak tree. A terrified kitten clung to one of the topmost branches.

I knocked on the neighbor's door, wondering how he could have been oblivious to these cries for the past three days. I explained the situation and he called his dogs into the house and told me I could use his aluminum extension ladder. I pulled it to its full height and leaned it against the tree. I don't like heights so I leaned inward toward the trunk as I climbed the wet metal steps.

When the cat saw help arriving, the cries became louder and it began to descend to lower branches. By the time I reached the last rung, five feet still separated me from the poor creature. "Kitty, I can't go any higher…it's now or never!" I said.

Understanding my message, the cat jumped and sank its claws into my shoulder, fortunately protected by Levi jacket and sweater beneath. I secured it with one hand, using the other to grip the ladder and cautiously backed down to the ground.

The cat still clung to me desperately as I carried the wet furry creature back to the house. I warmed up a plate of milk that it devoured, then walked to a nearby store and purchased a few cans of cat food and hurried back to feed it more. Soon it was asleep. When it awoke, it climbed onto my lap.

Next day, I left the house and began to walk to the post office but the cat would not let me out of its sight and followed me. While I went inside to check my mail, it waited outside by the door. Then it followed me home.

A week later I woke with a severe pain in my neck. I was usually in excellent health and was puzzled by this unexpected malady. I lay moaning, face down on the futon, when the cat came and lay across my neck and began purring. In a few minutes the pain was gone. I sat up and looked into the cat's eyes. There seemed to be a recognition of a bond that was beyond words.

My Reserved Space

I used to drive to Ashland to see the Shakespeare plays. This small town in Oregon a little over an hour from Mount Shasta, had four theaters, one of them an outdoor Elizabethan stage. People came from far and wide to attend the performances, go to day spas, and dine in the excellent restaurants, so it was hard to find a parking place. Even though they built several multi-story garages to handle the overflow of vehicles, they were often filled.

I drove north one day to see a play and I decided to put the I AM teachings to use and manifest a place to park. Turning my focus inward, I repeated three times silently, *I am the Presence of God bringing me the perfect parking place.*

As I entered town I sensed where that space would be and slowed down as I approached. Sure enough, it was, right where I had seen. I parked with satisfaction that the great law of energy had worked as it must, and went to enjoy the play.

I used this method every time I went to Ashland and the same place was always available. After a while, so I wouldn't have to say the words each time, I reserved the parking space permanently by affirming, *I am the Presence reserving the parking place for me permanently whenever I need it.* From then on, it was always there, waiting as surely as though it had a "reserved" sign.

After my three year retreat in the Catskill Mountains of New York, I came back to Mount

Shasta. I decided one day to go to Ashland to avail myself of the large food co-op and visit the metaphysical bookstore, Sound Peace, which stocked the books I had written.

I had forgotten about the congested parking until I drove into town. It was a weekend and the traffic was heavy, without a parking place in sight. As I drove down the main street, there was my old parking space where it had always been. Despite my absence, it was still reserved.

Embracing Life as the Path

After Pearl left her body, I felt the inner guidance to continue the study of Vajrayanna Buddhism I had begun with Trungpa Rinpoche in 1971. This guidance manifested further when Chugdud Rinpoche appeared in a dream and told me to come see him.[27] He was holding a nine-day Vajrasattva retreat at his ashram in Junction City, a three-hour drive from Mount Shasta. The practice changed my life, and after I returned home, I continued to practice daily in my shrine room.

Vajrasattva is the meditational Deity (Sanskrit: *yiddam*) that creates all other Deities—in other words, God, manifesting as your I AM Presence. Vajrasattva dissolves into a ball of golden light emitting rainbow colors, then enters your heart—and you realize "I am Vajrasattva." I was stunned to find the I AM teachings hidden in the ancient texts of Tibetan Buddhism.

At the end of the practice you dissolve the visualization and return to self-awareness; however, you can maintain the image of the Deity still above your head, sending out blessings throughout the day. Some Christians do a similar practice by visualizing Jesus or Mary overhead.

---

[27] Ascension can be completed on a higher plane after the death of the physical body. Read the fascinating autobiography of Chagdud Tulku Rinpoche in *Lord of the Dance: The Autobiography of a Tibetan Lama* (Padma Publishing, 2014).

I heard from a Buddhist friend one day about a reincarnated teacher known as a *tulku,* who was going to teach at Pema Osel Ling, the retreat center in the mountains east of Santa Cruz.[28] I felt drawn to study with him. However, I was now taking care of my eighty-five year old mother who had come to live with me, and I did not want to leave her alone. The solution was to have a friend's daughter stay at the house while I was gone; however, I would never have left home if I had known the life changing events that were about to happen.

At the retreat center, the cabin I was given among the trees on the mountain hillside was the ideal place to meditate. I rose before sunrise to turn my attention inward, then went to the temple to participate in Buddhist practices led by the head lama. Then came breakfast, followed by personal instruction from the tulku.

I began to learn Tibetan Astrology from the tulku. Amazingly, a person's hand can be used as an astrology chart. From this, one can discover what spiritual practices are most appropriate at that particular time in one's life. After looking at the planetary configurations in my palm he concluded I had an inauspicious aspect. When I expressed

---

[28]*Tulku,* a Tibetan term for a highly advanced soul who reincarnates to continue his work, usually recognized by Lamas who knew him previously or whose inner sight allows them this ability. However, when they can't find the right one someone else is named to fill the gap.

dismay over this revelation, he said, "Don't worry, the Dalai Lama has the same aspect."

He then explained that rather than the aspect being negative, it could be interpreted to mean I had a mission in life that could only be accomplished by doing spiritual practice. Practice was the Tibetan answer for everything. In fact, they rejoiced in inauspicious aspects, for that gave them the incentive to perform rituals that would transmute negativity into wisdom. The long Tibetan winters gave them a great opportunity to turn their attention inward and develop the mind—and attain enlightenment. In the West the tendency is more toward finding distractions that enable one to avoid looking inward at the true self.

Being an astrologer myself, I asked him if he would like me to look at his western chart. He agreed but was shocked to hear that the Saturn and Venus square clearly indicated he had lessons to learn about relationship. When I mentioned this challenge, he pushed the chart away and said he didn't want to hear any more.

Since he was about to attend college in Santa Cruz to improve his English, I knew he would soon encounter women who would be sure to teach him about relationship. He seemed to have dropped out of the Buddhist limelight and I wonder if he later renounced his monk's vows and became a householder.[29] Certainly, any challenge not dealt with in this life will become a seed bearing fruit in a subsequent life.

I worked on my own challenge the tulku had seen depicted in my planets, and did the Sanskrit mantra, meditation, and offerings he said were indicated. These made me happy, and when I wasn't in class or in the temple, I was by myself working on these practices. I was determined to dissolve all negativity and achieve the fulfillment of my destiny. Little did I suspect that my destiny was soon to assert itself in a way then unanticipated.

One morning there was a knock at the cabin door and a woman from the office said I had received an important phone call. This was before cell phones, so I went back to the office to call the number I had been given. I found myself speaking to a friend who said my former wife had experienced a heart attack. I had to return to Mount Shasta immediately to take care of my nine-year old daughter. Now I had to become full-time care giver for my nine-year-old daughter— a role that continued until she left home years later.

I was stunned. I was becoming a monk in order to pursue enlightenment full-time. I had no interest in remaining enmeshed in *samsara,* the pursuit of ever-changing phenomena that lead to suffering. However, soon I was back in my mother's house in

---

[29] Recently, I discovered that he had, in fact, married and has children.

Mount Shasta, where my distraught daughter awaited my return.

I became a full-time parent. Taking care of my mother and daughter at the same time proved harder than I imagined. In addition to catering to their various dietary preferences, I cleaned house, did laundry, and shopped for groceries—formerly the work of what in my youth was called a housewife. I remembered the saying I had seen on a friend's refrigerator, "A man's work is from sun to sun—a woman's work is never done." Now I understood.

After washing the dishes one day and watching the soapy water swirl down the drain, I felt that symbolized my life going down the drain as well. I had wanted to practice Buddhism, yet here I was just taking care of people. Only later did I realize that caring for others is the very heart of Buddhism (as well as Christianity).

At that moment a realization exploded in my mind: *I am where I need to be! Tantra uses everything as the path. Instead of seeing my mother and daughter as obstacles, I will see them as Deities here to advance me on the path to liberation!*

I said inwardly,

From now on, I am seeing my mother and daughter as Goddesses here to teach me what I need. May all that I do for them benefit all mothers and daughters everywhere.

I vowed that I would use daily life to attain Mastery. In fact, by taking care of my family, I might advance more rapidly than if I became a monk in an ashram. Hadn't Yogananda's guru, Sri Yukteswar and his guru, Lahiri Mahasaya, also been householders? I was in good company. It is hard enough to achieve enlightenment in a cave where you never have to deal with people, but to achieve mastery in the midst of human existence—was more difficult—but also far more rewarding in the end. I saw that Mastery is the next step beyond enlightenment. While visualizing both women as Deities, I recited various Goddess mantras and tantric practice became the framework of life.

Unexpectedly, my mother began to lose her appetite and finally stopped eating. She refused to go to the hospital as she felt no pain and didn't trust doctors; she'd had two surgeries to remove lumps from her lungs, and her surgeon had confessed it was the first operation itself that had caused the cancer to spread.

Since we had a meditation group that did the Medicine Buddha practice at the house every Thursday night, we moved the meeting into her bedroom. We sat in a semi-circle around her bed, chanted the Medicine Buddha mantra, and visualized her as the Medicine Buddha. She became transformed in our minds into a Deity of lapis blue light, radiating healing rays out to all sentient beings. Although she didn't understand what we were doing, she none-the-less enjoyed our company. By the third week, although she had been an atheist her whole life, she would occasionally point upward and ask, "Who are those beautiful beings of Light?

At the end of our meditation, when everyone filed out of the room and bowed to her, she held up her hands and blessed everyone.

Before she died, I felt I needed to talk to her. I didn't know the protocol for saying goodbye to your dying mother, but I felt I had to clear feelings I still had from childhood. I had felt like a failure most of my life, at least in her eyes. She had wanted me to be a professional, a doctor or lawyer that she could feel proud of when talking to her friends. Instead, I had wandered around the world. She had to say to her friends with great embarrassment, "He's still searching for himself…He hasn't found his niche yet."

I finally confessed at her bedside, "Mom, I'm sorry I wasn't a better son."

She looked at me and said with great tenderness, "You have been the perfect son, the best son I could have asked for. I'm just sorry I wasn't a better mother."

"Mom, you were the perfect mother."

"Really?"

"Yes, Mom," I said, for I realized now that it was the very struggle to find my own identity that had forced me to search, to embark on the lifelong quest to find the reality that was free of illusion.

That was the last conversation we had. She left her body the next morning as the sun rose.

My mother, age twenty-one.

My Mother Returns

Twenty years after my mother died, I woke from a nap one afternoon and sensed her presence. At first, I thought it might be one of the Deities I visualized as part of my tantric practice, for it was a loving, maternal presence, while in life she had seemed cold and unfeeling. I sat up and saw it truly was my mother, only now she was as beautiful as she had been as a young woman. Knowing she would not appear for a trivial purpose, I asked, "Mom, what can I do for you?"

"I need for you to forgive me," she said.

"Of course, I forgive you…didn't I forgive you on your deathbed?"

"No, I mean really forgive. Saint Germain has told me that I cannot progress in my evolution and that he cannot take me to a higher level until you let go of your pain."

I thought that I had let go of those issues a long time ago, but I now saw that some emotional wounds were still there, and I had further work to do. I saw you cannot simply decree feelings out of existence. They are interwoven with all aspects of our being and need to be brought to the surface, looked at, understood, and dissolved. Only then can we be free.

Our evolution is inextricably connected. Although she had been responsible for my death in past lives, in this one she had given me life. To raise me as best she knew how had been the focus of her life. Now she could advance no further until I let go of past wounds.

I thought about what had made her the way she was. I realized how cruel her own parents had been. Her mother had believed she was a descendent of Catherine the Great of Russia, so had tried to live like an aristocrat. She hired governesses to raise her daughter, frequently poor girls escaping the famine in Ireland. Some would only stay a year before running off. No wonder she had grown up wounded, feeling rejected by her mother, and not knowing how to be a mother herself.

Who knows, perhaps I had hurt her in a previous life? In any case, karmic lessons had arisen, and their emotional wounds needed to be healed. I realized, *Perhaps I am the one who caused her coldness by something I once did and that I no longer remember. Or, I might have caused a similar wound in someone else and, in order to cure that tendency, needed to reap the consequences? I could not have been born to this woman if it were not the consequence of my own previous actions.*

I let go of my victimhood and took responsibility for myself, realizing, *I am the cause of everything in my life.*

I felt suddenly free. A wave of forgiveness and compassion washed through my heart. I asked Saint Germain to grant my mother liberation…to take her to the higher world he had shown her. I knew someday we would meet again…as dear friends.

Three months later my mother appeared again, this time accompanied by her mother, Hannah, who ascended in my youth. They both wore white robes and had their arms around each other's shoulders. They smiled with great love and compassion, and my mother said, "Thank you for releasing me. I am now free…and so are you."

The two beautiful lady masters, who in Tibet would have been called dakinis, then disappeared. I feel them draw close occasionally, to help when the need arises.

Saint Germain Sends a Helper

As I sat at my desk writing, I received a phone call from Lillian at the Herb and Health store in town. She asked me to come down and sign a copy of my autobiographical book, *Apprentice to the Masters: Adventures of a Western Mystic, Book II,* for a woman from Switzerland by the name of Mona Stein who was on a pilgrimage to the mountain.

After I signed the book, I wished Mona a good visit to the Mountain, then returned home to continue writing—thinking I would never see her again. However, next day Mona phoned and asked if she could make an appointment. As she was leaving town soon, I said come right up.

She sat on the edge of the sofa recounting the chain of events that brought her to Mount Shasta. She had read *Unveiled Mysteries*, the story of Guy Ballard's meeting with Saint Germain on Mount Shasta, and the next morning on waking heard, "Go to Mount Shasta."

She went to a travel agent and after a great deal of searching they located Mount Shasta on a map. The agent was horrified, "Oh, dear, you don't want to go to that place…there are no tourist attractions whatsoever! Let me arrange a trip to Hawaii. You can go sightseeing in San Francisco for a few days, then go on to Maui."

"But I heard 'Go to Mount Shasta,'" Mona persisted.

The agent relented slightly, still setting up the trip to Maui, but leaving enough time in San Francisco for a three-day excursion to Mount Shasta. Now here she was, clutching my book with the cover of me wielding the Sword of Blue Flame.[30]

"Yesterday, when I went back to the motel and opened your book, I heard the same voice that told me to come to Mount Shasta. It scared me, so I threw the book under the bed. This morning I fished it out and heard it again. This time it was more specific. I don't want to scare you, but the voice said that you and I have work to do together."

"What! Are you sure?" I asked, incredulous.

"Yes, I'm sure. I think I'm supposed to translate your book into German and bring you to Europe to present the teachings of the Masters there."

"That would be amazing," I replied.

"It's settled then, I will leave tomorrow and when I'm back in Switzerland we can discuss the details," she said.

She threw her arms around me and bounded out the door to her car. As she headed down the road she waved, excitedly. A week later she phoned from Switzerland, saying she had set up talks for me in Switzerland and Germany, so I scheduled a flight.

This was only one of the many times Saint Germain inspired people to miraculously offer help in disseminating his teachings.

---

[30] This image is symbolic of Manjusri, the Lord of Wisdom, wielding the sword of discriminating intelligence. It is also symbolic of the Sword of Blue Flame of Archangel Michael—the purpose of this image being to inspire people to cut through the ignorance in their own lives.

Latte Art

I was given an Italian espresso machine by a dear friend who is a coffee aficionado. He not only produced a shot of supreme espresso but adorned the surface of his lattes with art, which is the master's touch that shows the care that permeates the entire creation. Practice as I might, I could not create the same hearts and flowers he produced. After years of trying, the best I could make was a cloud of foam.

Is there a message in this failure? I asked myself one day. *What am I not doing that I usually do to be successful?*

I realized that I had been relying on my friend's instructions and the numerous online videos for guidance, rather than calling on the I AM Presence. I didn't want to bother God for such a trifling matter as a foam design on the surface of a cup of coffee. Then again, why not? God is above me with unlimited power, aware of everything I do, and capable of working miracles. Next morning, I said,

*I Am the Presence of God
creating the perfect design.*

After frothing the milk, I took the small metal pot in my right hand and, emptying my mind, allowed the milk to flow out however it wanted. To my great surprise, on the surface of the coffee was the Chinese character for victory, which I recognized from studying Qi Gong. The teacher, Larry Wong, had explained that the actual meaning of the pictograph is:

Fall down six times…get up seven.

I had fallen down a thousand times, but on the thousand and first I was successful. When I got my mind out of the way, the perfect design just happened….

I Am God

On New Year's Eve the Masters release an outpouring of Light to the planet. Frequently I would awaken the following morning charged with energy and know my work for the year ahead.

This New Year's Day, a woman with many questions came to visit: "Why am I here? How can I support myself? She thought I had the answers, so I closed my eyes and said silently to myself,

*I am the Presence of God
helping this person!*

Suddenly and without warning, I became God. I was seated on a throne at the center of the Universe, radiating infinite rays of light. Galaxies whirled past and I knew that all was an emanation of myself. I opened my eyes and, although the woman and the room were still there, the backdrop was infinity. Trying to maintain a presence in the human reality, I said, "Your problems are your own creation…they are not real!"

"But…but…but" she stammered.

I realized she wanted to feel she was a victim of circumstance rather than to take charge of her life. She wanted many things, all without having to work to attain money to buy them. She wanted God to end her suffering. As God, I could fix everything for her, but knew she had created this situation to realize that she too was God.

Then I saw why Neem Karoli Baba had refused to be my Guru. I had to find the Guru within myself. He could not do that for me. Nor could I now do that for this woman. By ignoring me for forty-five years, Neem Karoli Baba had given me the greatest teaching. As I looked at the suffering woman before me, I realized that once I would have felt impatience, but now I felt compassion.

"Look, you are God. Use your Divine Intelligence and Divine Will to create your life as you wish," I said. but it was like talking to a mannequin and she only stared dumbly back.

I allowed me eyes to close and remembered entering duality ages ago, as though volunteering to play a virtual reality game. What the Bible called The Fall was only a fall from oneness into duality—the experience of good and bad, pleasure and pain, right and wrong—all for the purpose of developing compassion. As I had learned what I wanted in this reality, I had emerged again into the oneness—to sit again on the Throne of God at the heart of Creation. It seemed to have taken a long time, but in eternity it had only been a moment.

A swelling glory within me began to envelop towns, continents, the earth, solar and stellar systems, tenuous nebulae, and the floating universes. The entire cosmos, gently luminous, like a city seen afar at night, glimmered within the infinitude of my being. -Paramahansa Yogananda

Dada Mukerjee (back), Peter Mt. Shasta, Ram Dass, Jai Uttal, Ganga Dhar, Maharajji (back).

The Crying Bowl

My life began to change in strange ways. I began to see that everything has consciousness and manifests a type of life. I never previously thought about having a conversation with an inanimate object; however, that experience was soon to become a reality.

I was preparing dinner one evening and reached into the cupboard for a bowl, when I heard a soft crying like that of a new-born kitten. I let go of the bowl and peered into the back of the cupboard. *What could be crying in there?* I wondered.

"Have you forgotten us?" came a plea from the corner of the shelf. "We want to be used too."

I had bought four blue porcelain bowls a few months ago and stacked them in the corner of the cupboard. When I prepared a meal, I always grabbed the top bowl, so the same bowl was used over and over while the others were ignored. It never occurred to me to take a bowl from the bottom of the pile. Now, I removed one of the neglected bowls and placed the well-used one on the bottom of the stack.

"Forgive me, I love you too," I said to the offended bowl. It seemed to glow with appreciation, grateful at finally being used for the purpose it had been created.

A Tree Being

We had a lot of fires that summer and fall and every few days my neighbor got out his chain saw and cut down another tree to make a fire break around his house. It was a good safety precaution, but I couldn't help feeling sorry for the trees that had sheltered his home for the past thirty years. They had lived in harmony, protected him and his family from the sun, and provided acorns for the squirrels and deer to eat during the winter.

It was going to snow soon and I decided to attach some red reflectors to trees along the 300-yard dirt driveway to my home in the forest, so that the man who plowed the driveway could see where to go. I went out with some heavy string and began tying the reflectors to the trees. I reached with both arms around each trunk to tie the knot in back.

Embracing the last tree, I was shocked to feel it light up and come to life. A wave of love entered my heart, and I saw that I was embracing a slender, luminous girl who lived within the tree. She seemed about seven years old and was radiantly joyful. When she began to speak, I was even more surprised: "I am so happy you are not going to cut me down like your neighbor."

A surge of energy leapt from my heart and, without thinking I blurted out, "I love you."

"I love you too," she replied.

I stepped back to look more closely at her, but now I could see only rough bark.

"I know you're in there. Please let me see you again," I pleaded, but she ignored the request. So, I went back inside.

A few days later there was a heavy snow. It turned bitterly cold and I woke in the middle of the night with a gnawing concern, *What about the girl in the tree? Is she cold? Perhaps I should give her a blanket and some warm tea?* But, as I woke more fully, I felt her saying, "I am fine. I do not feel cold but thank you for thinking of me. Come visit me sometime."

I went back to sleep and in the morning thought of her again, sitting silently out there in the forest by herself. As a hermit, I sometimes felt lonely. Now I knew there was a loving being nearby. In fact, as I looked out my window into the forest, I realized that every tree was embodied by a similar being, so I was hardly alone.

Dog Wisdom

It had been a hard morning. I had received some challenging emails about business and had also seen news that sounded as though humanity was doomed. Instead of processing all this in meditation as usual, I climbed in my truck and headed toward town. Suddenly, a dog appeared in the middle of the road a few hundred yards ahead. I tapped the horn a few times, but the dog did not move. He remained with all four paws planted firmly on the road and as he watched me approach. I slowed down, expecting him to step to the side, but the huge, black dog with an orange spot on the top of his head remained motionless, staring at me through the windshield.

I stopped the truck finally and he ambled over to the side window. I rolled it down and held out my hand and he gently placed his muzzle in my palm. As he looked soulfully into my eyes, my anxiety departed and I felt at peace. In some way he had communicated a powerful message.

He then backed away and allowed me to pass. As I drove on down the road toward town, I now felt everything was going to work out. It was a beautiful day with a clear blue sky and the sun shone brightly overhead.

Disappearing Wasps

I was stung by a wasp, but it was my fault as I was chanting the *Gayatri* mantra and inadvertently backed into the post on which the wasp was resting. Rather than blame him, I was concerned about his wellbeing and watched as he smoothed himself from the abrupt encounter. The next day I found another wasp trapped between the window and screen, and carefully scooped it into a container and put it outside in the grass. When my landlord heard I had been stung, she offered to spray poison, but the idea was abhorrent. I wondered what to do.

In the evening I went outside onto the deck. Looking overhead, I saw the three wasp nests that were under construction under the eaves of the roof. I had watched the nests grow larger every day. As they buzzed about their work I looked up and said, *I know you are a part of Mother Nature and need a place to live, but I also need a place to live. Now is the time for you to relocate. You have until tomorrow morning. If you are still there then, I will use the hose to knock you down with a jet of water. If that doesn't work, I will let my landlord use poison.*

I went to sleep that night knowing I would have to get up early in the morning while the air was still cold and the wasps were dormant.

I woke before sunrise, dreading the encounter ahead, and quickly dressed. I went outside and got the hose and carried it upstairs to the porch where

I could reach the roof, then went back down to turn on the water. As the sun's rays began to come over the tree tops and illuminate the eaves of the roof, I looked up. The wasps were gone…and they never returned.

The Book Title

Originally, the title of this book was clear, the one I had intuited, but after a while I began to doubt, *perhaps there is a better title?* Over time, I changed the title more than a dozen times. Every time I opened the file to write, a new name popped into mind. Finally, in frustration I prayed to Saint Germain to show me the title he wanted.

I went to Seven Suns Café next day for a bowl of soup, which I ate outside on the patio. After I finished, I walked back out to the sidewalk. A young man passed and as he went by, he looked back over his shoulder at me and said, "It is what it is."

I turned for a second to say goodbye to a friend on the patio, then looked back to see who this man was—but there was no one there.

Whose Game Is It?

You created the game, but don't remember when you chose to participate as a player. Everything in the game is an illusion, created and sustained for your expansion and enlightenment. Pleasure and pain, good and evil, right and wrong, are all polarities needed as rules for the game. The game seems real because you forgot who you are. Remember, and the game ends. You are an immortal being dwelling in eternity.

No Obstacles!

Sky is sky; rock is rock; earth is earth; mountains are mountains. I am what I am, and you are what you are. Therefore, there are no particular obstacles to experiencing our world....

-Chögyam Trungpa Rinpoche,
The Tantric Path of Indestructible Wakefulness

www.ingramcontent.com/pod-product-compliance
Lightning Source LLC
Chambersburg PA
CBHW070601010526
44118CB00012B/1412